Best Editorial Cartoons of the Year

D1537020

JOHN KNUDSEN
Courtesy The Tidings

MIDDLE EAST STRIFE

ARABS ISRAELIS

AND THEY CALL THIS THE HOLY LAND!

TIMER

BEST EDITORIAL CARTOONS OF THE YEAR

1989 EDITION

Edited by
CHARLES BROOKS

PELICAN PUBLISHING COMPANY
GRETNA 1989

Library of Congress Serial Catalog Data

Best editorial cartoons. 1972-
   Gretna [La.] Pelican Pub. Co.
   v. 29 cm. annual-
"A pictorial history of the year."

   1. United States- Politics and government—
1969—Caricatures and Cartoons—Periodicals.
E839.5.B45   320.9'7309240207   73-643645
ISSN 0091-2220   MARC-S

Manufactured in the United States of America
Published by Pelican Publishing Company, Inc.
1101 Monroe Street, Gretna, Louisiana 70053

Contents

Award-Winning Cartoons

1988 PULITZER PRIZE

MARLETTE ©1987
THE ATLANTA CONSTITUTION

"PRESIDENT?... NO, CHILD, BUT YOU CAN GROW UP TO BE FRONT-RUNNER!"

DOUG MARLETTE
Editorial Cartoonist
Atlanta Constitution

Native of Greensboro, North Carolina; began drawing cartoons for newspapers at age 16; attended Florida State University, majoring in philosophy and minoring in art; editorial cartoonist for the *Charlotte Observer,* 1972–87; editorial cartoonist for the *Atlanta Constitution,* 1987 to the present; only cartoonist to be awarded a Nieman Fellowship to Harvard; five book collections of his works have been published; winner of numerous awards for cartooning.

1988 NATIONAL HEADLINERS CLUB AWARD

"THAT'S RIGHT— JIM AND TAMMY WERE EXPELLED FROM PARADISE AND LEFT ME IN CHARGE!"

DOUG MARLETTE

Editorial Cartoonist

Charlotte Observer

1987 NATIONAL SOCIETY OF PROFESSIONAL JOURNALISTS AWARD
(Selected in 1988)

TAMMY AND JIM, FACING HUGE DEFICITS AND UNDER FIRE FROM THE RIGHT WING, RELAXING AT THEIR HOME IN CALIFORNIA.

PAUL CONRAD
Editorial Cartoonist
Los Angeles Times

Earned degree in art, University of Iowa, 1950; editorial cartoonist for the *Denver Post,* 1950–63; editorial cartoonist for the *Los Angeles Times,* 1964 to the present; cartoons syndicated by the Los Angeles Times Syndicate; named a fellow of the Society of Professional Journalists, 1986; winner of numerous awards for cartooning, including three Pulitzer Prizes.

1987 NATIONAL NEWSPAPER AWARD / CANADA
(Selected in 1988)

RAFFI ANDERIAN
Editorial Cartoonist
Ottawa Citizen

Graduate of Sheridan College, Toronto, 1985; editorial cartoonist for the *Ottawa Citizen,* 1986 to the present; at age 24, youngest person ever to win the National Newspaper Award of Canada for editorial cartooning.

1988 FISCHETTI AWARD

YOU FOOLED AROUND
ZOT
YOU PLAGIARIZED
ZOT
AND YOU SMOKED POT
ZOT
BOY, I'M GLAD I NEVER DID ANY OF THAT STUFF.
WIMP
ZOT
BOK

ARTHUR BOK

Editorial Cartoonist

Akron Beacon Journal

Graduate of the University of Dayton, 1974; editorial cartoonist for the *Clearwater* (Fla.) *Sun,* 1981–82; editorial cartoonist for *Tropic,* Sunday magazine of the *Miami Herald,* 1983–86; editorial cartoonist for the *Akron Beacon Journal,* 1986 to the present.

1988 INTERNATIONAL SALON OF CARTOONS AWARD

HIGGINS

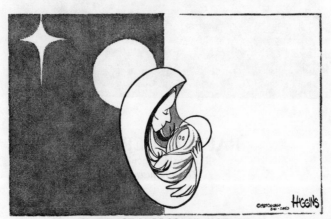

THE FIRST SURROGATE MOTHER

JACK HIGGINS

Editorial Cartoonist

Chicago Sun-Times

Native of Chicago; graduate of Holy Cross College, Worcester, Mass.; editorial cartoonist for the *Chicago Sun-Times,* 1981 to the present; only American to receive an award in the 1988 International Salon of Cartoons, which attracted some 3,000 entrants.

Best Editorial Cartoons of the Year

I pledge allegiance to the flag
of the United States of America,
and the Republic of Panama with which we stand;
Iran-Contra, through Noriega, covert aid,
with cocaine and weapons for all.

PAUL CONRAD
Courtesy Los Angeles Times

12

The Republican Campaign

Vice-President George Bush began the 1988 campaign for the Republican nomination as the front-runner, and as the year began there appeared to be only two opponents who had a chance of overtaking him—Senator Robert Dole of Kansas and former television evangelist Pat Robertson. Representative Jack Kemp, Governor Pierre DuPont, and former Secretary of State Alexander Haig were not able to mount strong campaigns.

Dole's candidacy began unraveling on March 5 when Bush won big in South Carolina's primary. Then, on Super Tuesday, Bush swept all sixteen states that held Republican primaries, and the nomination was his.

Massachusetts Governor Michael Dukakis held a strong lead in national polls following the Democratic convention in July. But after the Republican convention in August, Bush began to climb and by early September had moved ahead in most polls. He stayed ahead, although some pollsters contended the race was close in the final days before the election.

Bush carried forty states with a total of 426 electoral votes while Dukakis collected only 112 electoral votes. Voters apparently had been satisfied with Ronald Reagan and saw Bush as an extension of Reagan.

THE PRESIDENT-ELECT AND RUNNING MATE

KEVIN SIERS
Courtesy Charlotte Observer

13

JOE HELLER
Courtesy Green Bay Press-Gazette

ON THE AIR

FOLKS... SOMETHING IS COMING OUT OF THE SPACESHIP! IT'S SHORT... WITH A BIG NOSE, SQUINTY EYES AND BIG BLACK EYEBROWS!! MY GAWD! IT'S A... IT'S A LIBERAL!!

THE WAR OF THE WORLDS PANIC - 50 years later

MIKE LANE
Courtesy Baltimore Evening Sun

STRATEGY

'THE SOUTH HAS RISEN AGAIN, BOYS... COMMENCE TO BURNING BROOKLINE AND DRIVE THE LIBERALS INTO THE SEA !!'

14

THE "L-WORD"!

DUKAKIS LOSES!

AND MANY THANKS TO WILLIE HORTON ... HOW 'BOUT AN INAUGURAL FURLOUGH?!

LINDA BOILEAU
Courtesy Frankfort State Journal

RALPH DUNAGIN
Courtesy Orlando Sentinel

"OH, NO! GEORGE COULDN'T EVEN REMEMBER WHEN THE DEMOCRATS BOMBED PEARL HARBOR!"

ROB ROGERS
Courtesy Pittsburgh Press

Boston Tea Party 1988

15

BOB GORRELL
Courtesy Richmond News-Leader

MIKE SMITH
Courtesy Las Vegas Sun

16

GARY MARKSTEIN
Courtesy Tribune Newspapers

AND DON'T COME OUT FOR FOUR YEARS!

QUAYLE

THE BUSH CABINET

PAUL SZEP
Courtesy Boston Globe

GEORGE HERBERT WALKER BUSH AND J. DANFORTH QUAYLE TO GO AFTER DUKAKIS 'LIKE A COUPLE OF PIT BULLS.'

LANDED THE BIG ONE —

NATIONAL POLL

ELECTION

DUKAKIS WATER

VALLEY TRIBUNE SHEVCHIK

JOHN SHEVCHIK
Courtesy Valley Tribune (Pa.)

THE FIRST THING I'D DO AFTER I BECAME PRESIDENT IS SAY A PRAYER.

SO WOULD WE!

QUAYLE

GEORGE FISHER
Courtesy Arkansas Gazette

DICK WALLMEYER
Courtesy Long Beach Press-Telegram

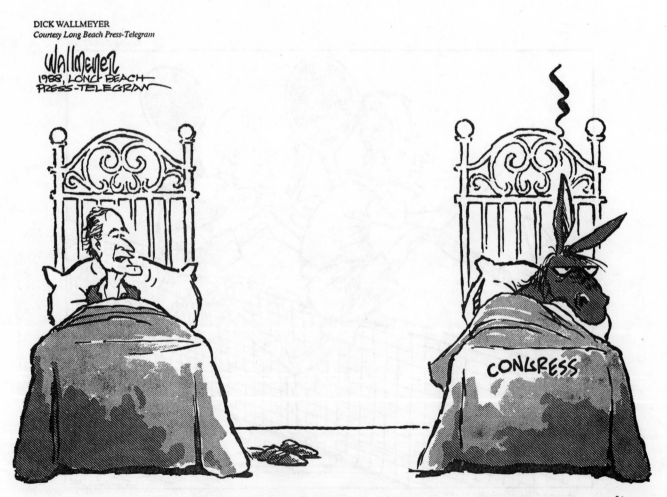

CONGRESS

"DOES THIS MEAN THERE WON'T BE A HONEYMOON?"

18

STEVE MCBRIDE
Courtesy Independence (Kan.) Daily Reporter

THE BENTSEN FASTBALL

Now that was a CHEAP SHOT...

You're in the Big League now, Dan!

DICK LOCHER
Courtesy Chicago Tribune

19

ENGELHARDT
©1993 St. Louis Post-Dispatch

TOM ENGELHARDT
Courtesy St. Louis Post-Dispatch

"I'VE RECENTLY BECOME AWARE OF THE NEED FOR CHILD-CARE"

LEN BOROZINSKI
Courtesy Phoenix Gazette

LAMBERT DER
Courtesy Greenville (S.C.) News

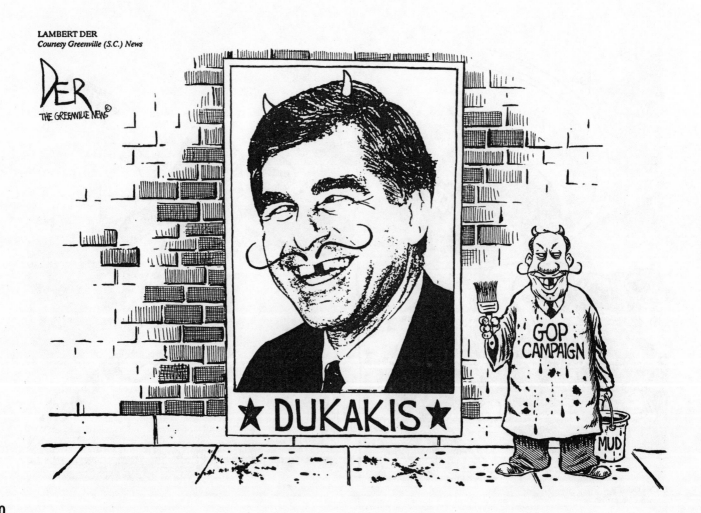

MIKE THOMPSON
Courtesy Thompson Cartoons

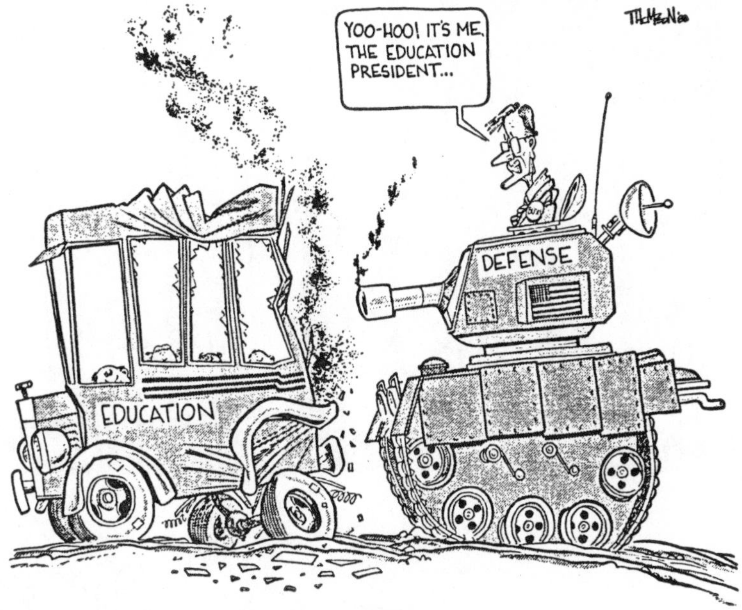
YOO-HOO! IT'S ME, THE EDUCATION PRESIDENT...
DEFENSE
EDUCATION

MIKE PETERS
Courtesy Dayton Daily News

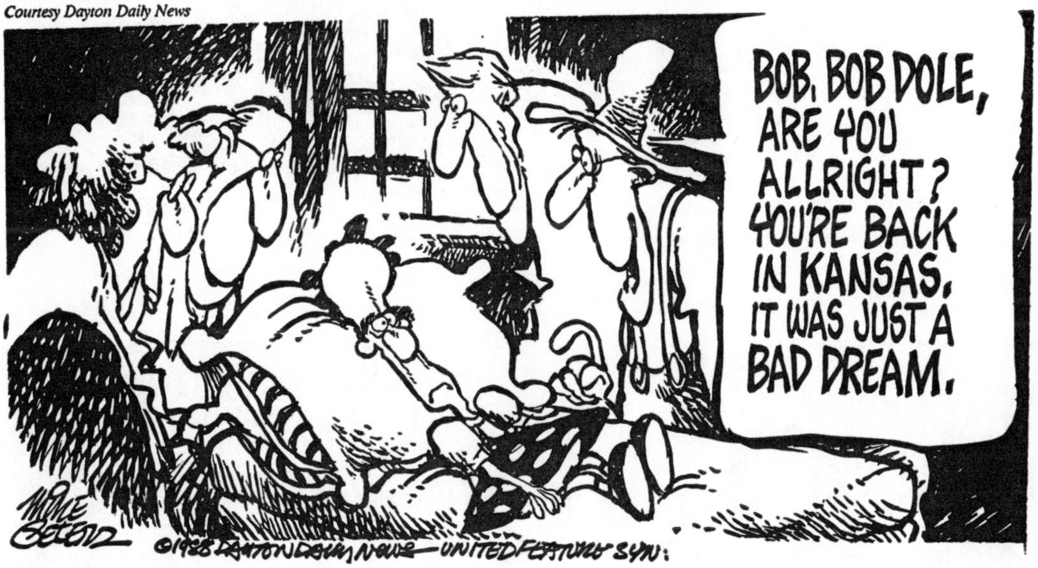
BOB, BOB DOLE, ARE YOU ALLRIGHT? YOU'RE BACK IN KANSAS. IT WAS JUST A BAD DREAM.

JACK HIGGINS
Courtesy Chicago Sun-Times

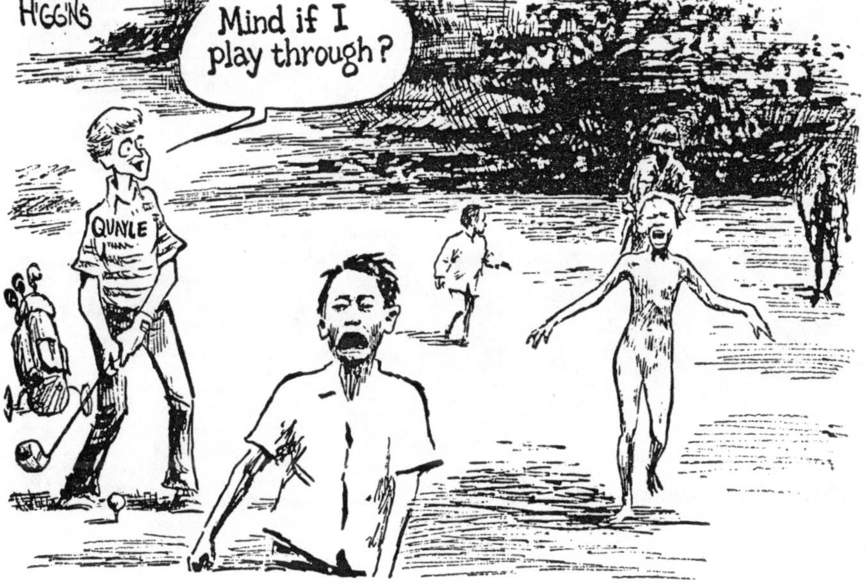
HIGGINS
Mind if I play through?
QUAYLE

DRUG WAR   DEFICITS   ENVIRONMENT   EDUCATION   ETHICS   HEALTH!

PLEDGE OF ALLEGIANCE ISSUE

GEORGE FISHER
Courtesy Arkansas Gazette

GEORGE SEEMS TO BE MAKING AN EFFORT!!

Yeah... but how do we know he's sincere?

BUSH MAKES PITCH FOR FEMALE VOTE!

ED GAMBLE
Courtesy Florida Times-Union

22

TESTY?'
I AM NOT TESTY, GORBACHEV!
YOU WANTA SEE TESTY, PAL?

PRESIDENT BUSH

THE BUTTON

BEN SARGENT
Courtesy Austin American-Statesman

THAT'S IT?
BUT WHAT
ABOUT THE
DEFICIT?
WHAT ABOUT
HEALTH
CARE?

CAN'T YOU
READ HIS
LIPS?

LET'S HEAR YOU
SAY THAT
PLEDGE,
NOW!

... I HOPE
THAT ISN'T
AN ACLU
CARD....

NOVEMBER MANDATE.....

KATE SALLEY PALMER
Courtesy Associated Features

23

"WHEW! THAT WAS CLOSE! A JOURNALIST ALMOST GOT TO HIM WITH A REAL QUESTION!"

BILL SANDERS
Courtesy Milwaukee Journal

"AND IF ELECTED I PROMISE I WON'T CUT DEFENSE, I WON'T RAISE TAXES AND I WON'T..."

...DIE.

SCOTT STANTIS
Courtesy Memphis Commercial Appeal

24

TO BE CONTINUED

"FOUR MORE YEARS!"

I WANT A KINDER, GENTLER NATION

BRIAN DUFFY
Courtesy Des Moines Register

26

The Democratic Campaign

The Seven Dwarfs, they were called—the name coined by the media to describe the field of candidates seeking the Democratic nomination for the presidency. Former Senator Gary Hart had dropped out of the race in 1987 after reports of extramarital affairs. He later reentered the race, but his campaign went nowhere. Senator Joseph Biden also withdrew early after being accused of resume-padding and plagiarism. One by one, the others fell—Senator Albert Gore, Jr., Governor Bruce Babbitt, Representative Richard Gephardt, Senator Paul Simon, and the Reverend Jesse Jackson.

Jackson had showed early strength in Illinois and Michigan, but Governor Michael Dukakis of Massachusetts turned the tide in Wisconsin and later sealed the nomination. Relations between Dukakis and Jackson were strained throughout the campaign, particularly after Dukakis failed to inform Jackson in advance of his selection of Senator Lloyd Bentsen as his running mate.

In the general election, Republican George Bush managed to hang the "liberal" label on Dukakis and charged him with running a huge deficit as governor and furloughing killers. The charges stuck and Dukakis managed to carry only nine states.

BOB GORRELL
Courtesy Richmond News-Leader

"OUCH!... AND WE THOUGHT DAN QUAYLE GOT LOUSY GRADES!..."

27

STEVE HILL
Courtesy Oklahoma Gazette

HE'S CALLED "THE CANDIDATE OF CHANGE"...

....BECAUSE IF HE GETS ELECTED, THAT'S ALL THAT WILL BE LEFT OF YOUR PAYCHECK...

..CHANGE!

TOM BECK
Courtesy Journal Standard (Ill.)

DICK LOCHER
Courtesy Chicago Tribune

OKAY— NOBODY TELLS HIM WHERE SNOW WHITE IS—

28

DANA SUMMERS
Courtesy Orlando Sentinel

YOU NEED SOME PERSONALITY, MIKE...SMILE!

NEVER MIND JUST BE YOURSELF.

MY FRIENDS, I'VE DONE A POOR JOB OF LETTING YOU KNOW THE **REAL** MIKE DUKAKIS.

I'VE LET OTHERS DEFINE ME. BUT NO LONGER.

I'M DEFINING ME. NO MORE LABELS. I'M ME AND I KNOW WHO I AM.

I'M HARRY TRUMAN!!

BUSH DEFEATS DUKAKIS

STUART CARLSON
Courtesy Milwaukee Sentinel

29

Well, we Democrats lost!

WE?

DICK LOCHER
Courtesy Chicago Tribune

JOHN DEERING
Courtesy Arkansas Democrat

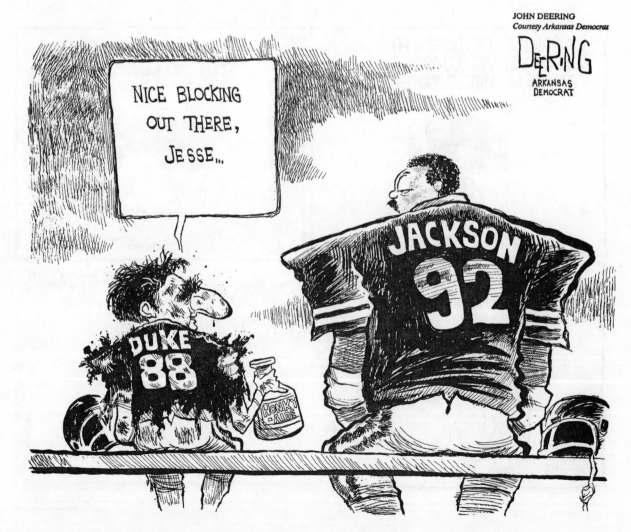

NICE BLOCKING OUT THERE, JESSE...

DUKE 88

HONKY-AIDE

JACKSON 92

30

CLAY BENNETT
Courtesy St. Petersburg Times

CHARLES BISSELL
Courtesy The Tennessean

ANOTHER FITTING PROBLEM

NICE OF YOU GUYS TO INVITE ME OUT FOR A RIDE – WHERE WE GOING?

JERRY FEARING
Courtesy St. Paul Pioneer Press-Dispatch

31

Chicago Daily Tribune

DUKAKIS DEFEATS DUKAKIS

JERRY BYRD
Courtesy Beaumont Enterprise

SPYDER WEBB
Courtesy Blade-Tribune

MR. DUKAKIS, COULD YOU CLARIFY YOUR FOREIGN POLICY POSITION FOR US?

CERTAINLY

32

CHUCK ASAY
Courtesy Colorado Springs
Gazette-Telegraph

PAYNE 10-11-88

EUGENE PAYNE
Courtesy Charlotte Observer

33

The L word

MIKE SMITH
Courtesy Las Vegas Sun

JOHN CRAWFORD
Courtesy Alabama Journal

life with robinson

JERRY ROBINSON
Courtesy Cartoonists and Writers Syndicate

34

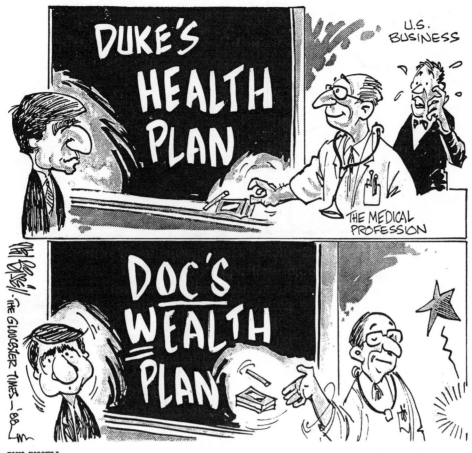

DUKE'S HEALTH PLAN

U.S. BUSINESS

THE MEDICAL PROFESSION

DOC'S WEALTH PLAN

PHIL BISSELL
Courtesy Gloucester Times

M. D. SHELTON
Courtesy Orange County Register

A LIBERAL IN THE FOOTSTEPS OF HARRY TRUMAN

WHY ISN'T IT WORKING?

STAHLER.
©THE CINCINNATI POST. 1988
NEA.

JEFF STAHLER
Courtesy Cincinnati Post

CRAIG MACINTOSH
Courtesy Minneapolis Star-Tribune

HOW WOULD YOU PAY FOR THAT PROGRAM, GOVERNOR?

DON'T FORGET IRAN-CONTRA!

WHAT ABOUT ABORTION?

REMEMBER NORIEGA!

AND YOUR IDEAS ON THE ECONOMY?

DON'T FORGET IRAN CONTRA!

WHAT'S YOUR FAVORITE COLOR?

REMEMBER NORIEGA!

IT'S NICE TO SEE WHERE YOU STAND ON SOMETHING, MIKE.

BRUCE TINSLEY '88 CHARLOTTESVILLE DAILY PROGRESS

BRUCE TINSLEY
Courtesy Charlottesville Daily Progress

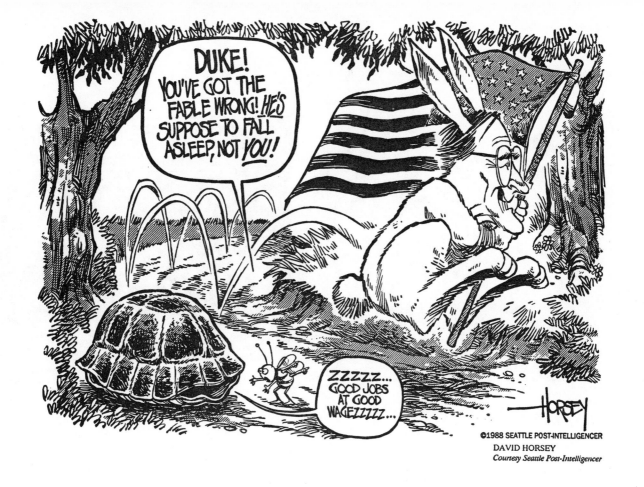

DUKE! YOU'VE GOT THE FABLE WRONG! HE'S SUPPOSE TO FALL ASLEEP, NOT *YOU*!

ZZZZZ... GOOD JOBS AT GOOD WAGEZZZZZ...

HORSEY

©1988 SEATTLE POST-INTELLIGENCER
DAVID HORSEY
Courtesy Seattle Post-Intelligencer

WAYNE STAYSKAL
Courtesy Tampa Tribune

EARTHQUAKE CENTER

STAYSKAL 88 TAMPA TRIBUNE

"WE LOCATED THE SOURCE OF THE TREMORS, CHIEF... IT'S JOHN WAYNE TURNING OVER IN HIS GRAVE EVERY TIME SOMEBODY CALLS DUKAKIS 'DUKE'!"

37

'THOSE WHO FAIL TO LEARN FROM HISTORY ARE DOOMED TO REPEAT THEIR MISTAKES.'

DUKAKIS — "LIBERALISM" — MONDALE — CARTER — McGOVERN

JIM LANGE
Courtesy Daily Oklahoman

THE LEGEND OF SUBSTANCE HOLLOW
or Ichabod Voter and the Headless Candidates

CHUCK AYERS
Courtesy Akron Beacon-Journal

ED STEIN
Courtesy Rocky Mountain News

ROCKY MTN. NEWS Ed Stein '88 NEA

JESSE, IT'S DUKAKIS. FORGET VICE PRESIDENT. WILL YOU ACCEPT SECRETARY OF CHARISMA?

38

The Reagan Administration

Two kiss-and-tell books by former White House aides contained unflattering revelations about President Reagan—and his wife Nancy. Former chief of staff Donald Regan wrote that Nancy consulted an astrologer regularly and that the president's schedule was influenced by the stars. Former press secretary Larry Speakes revealed that on several occasions he had made up quotes that he attributed to Reagan.

The INF Treaty, the first pact between the U.S. and the Soviet Union to eliminate an entire class of nuclear weapons, was ratified by the Senate after Reagan and Russia's Mikhail Gorbachev had reached agreement the previous December. Effective June 1, 1988, all U.S. and Soviet missiles with a range of up to 3,400 miles were to be eliminated within three years. Related facilities also were to be dismantled, and compliance was to be ensured by satellite and unprecedented on-site inspections.

It was widely believed that President Reagan would pardon Lt. Col. Oliver North and John Poindexter, the former national security advisor, for their roles in the Iran/Contra affair. The president, however, said that to issue a pardon would suggest that the two had committed a crime, and Reagan felt strongly that they had not.

FRANK EVERS
Courtesy New York Post

39

SPLENDID! A RUNNING HEAD START ON MY WELFARE REFORM

$44 BILLION SUPER COLLIDER PROJECT GOES TO TEXAS

DRAPER HILL
Courtesy Detroit News

WALT HANDELSMAN
Courtesy Scranton Times

MADAME NANCY'S
• PALM READING
• TAROT CARDS
• CRYSTAL BALL
• ASTROLOGY
POLITICAL FORTUNES TOLD HERE!

...GOSH, NANCY, WHEN YOU SAID YOU WERE CONSULTING THE STARS, I THOUGHT YOU WERE JUST CALLING OUR OLD MOVIE PALS!

S. C. RAWLS
Courtesy NEA

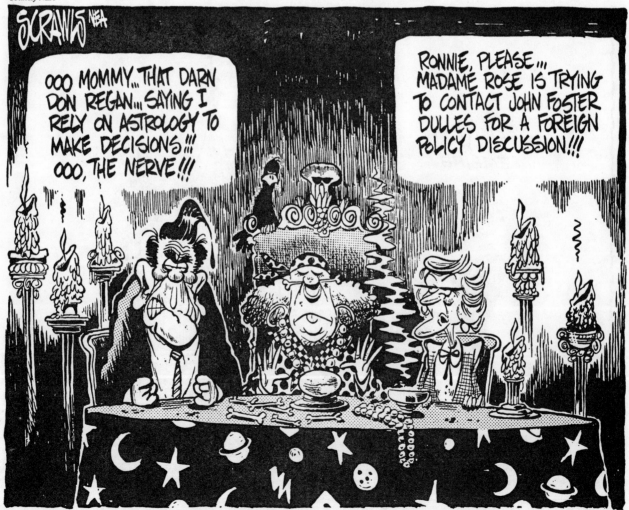

SCRAWLS NEA

OOO MOMMY...THAT DARN DON REGAN....SAYING I RELY ON ASTROLOGY TO MAKE DECISIONS !!! OOO, THE NERVE !!!

RONNIE, PLEASE .... MADAME ROSE IS TRYING TO CONTACT JOHN FOSTER DULLES FOR A FOREIGN POLICY DISCUSSION !!!

40

RAY OSRIN
Courtesy Cleveland Plain Dealer

WHEN THE MOON IS IN THE 7th HOUSE...

AND JUPITER ALIGNS WITH MARS...

THE MAMA AND THE PAPA

TOM GIBB
Courtesy Altoona Mirror

©1988, ALTOONA MIRROR

THE WORST THING ABOUT THIS DON REGAN BOOK IS THE FEELING THAT ANYONE AROUND ME MIGHT BETRAY ME. ...NOW, THAT'S A SILLY NOTION, I KNOW...

PSSSST....HELLO, DOUBLEDAY?

41

HY ROSEN
Courtesy Albany Times-Union

"LEAVE IT TO DEAVER"

PERSONAL APPOINTMENTS SECRETARY

HE'LL SEE YOU WHEN *VENUS* AND *MARS* ARE IN *CAPRICORN*!

OVAL OFFICE

JIM LANGE
Courtesy Daily Oklahoman

BY GOLLY..THAT'S A GREAT QUOTE! WHO SAID IT?

YOU DID, MR. PRESIDENT.

JOHN CRAWFORD
Courtesy Alabama Journal

42

I'VE DECIDED I DON'T WANT TO DEAL ANYMORE

NORIEGA

BOB TAYLOR
Courtesy Dallas Times-Herald

RING! RING! RING! RING! RING! RING! RING!

OLLIE NORTH PARDON

DICK WRIGHT
Courtesy Providence Journal-Bulletin

43

STEVE SACK
Courtesy Minneapolis Star-Tribune

THE PIED PIPER

DAVID MARTIN
Courtesy Sun Newspapers

BRUCE BEATTIE
Courtesy Daytona Beach News-Journal

"Uh, Ron, the sunset you're supposed to ride off into is THAT way..."

© Majeski '88 TIMES LEADER

BOLSHOI BALLET ANYONE?

NUKE-EM

HOMO EVILEMPIRUS REAGANUS 1983

HOMO SUMMITUS REAGANUS 1988

—— EVOLUTION ——

WAKE UP, MR. PRESIDENT, YOUR EIGHT YEAR TERMS ARE UP!

TV PROGRAMS

THE JELLY BEANS, JIM, DON'T FORGET THE JELLY BEANS!

Angulo 88

THE DAY REAGAN LEAVES OFFICE

SENATOR, YOU'RE NO JACK KENNEDY...

SEN. QUAYLE

THANK GOD!

JOHN CRAWFORD
Courtesy Alabama Journal

STUART CARLSON
Courtesy Milwaukee Sentinel

I AM, TOO, PRESIDENTIAL! I AM! I AM! JUST ASK MY...UM...MOM AND DAD! OR MY MATERNAL GRANDMOTHER — SHE'S EVEN OLDER THAN LLOYD HERE. AND I'D KNOW THE CABINET BY NAME ...UM... I'D EVEN KNOW NICKNAMES! I COULD HANDLE IT...REALLY I COULD!...ASK ANYONE...

Quayle

Bentsen

46

Politics / The Debates

The year 1988 was filled with charges against judges, politicians, high-level public officials, and the Pentagon. Attorney General Edwin Meese resigned in the wake of charges that he had traded government jobs for financial favors, and two former advisors to President Reagan—Michael Deaver and Lyn Nofziger—were prosecuted on charges of illegal lobbying.

The Pentagon was hit with bribery and fraud allegations involving defense contracts worth billions of dollars. Arizona Governor Evan Mecham was impeached and removed from office, Senator Joseph Biden was forced from the presidential race after being accused of plagiarism, and Florida federal judge Alcee Hastings was impeached for an alleged bribery conspiracy.

The Bush-Dukakis television debates enlivened the political scene somewhat, offering each candidate the possibility of delivering a knockout punch. It was generally agreed that Dukakis narrowly won the first debate and Bush swept the second. Dukakis's running mate, Lloyd Bentsen, bested Republican vice-presidential candidate Senator Dan Quayle in their only televised debate. Bentsen's most memorable line: "Senator, you're no Jack Kennedy."

GENE BASSET
Courtesy Atlanta Journal

BEFORE THE DEBATE

AFTER THE DEBATE

47

STEVE ARTLEY
Courtesy Agri News

AGRI NEWS•ROCHESTER•MN

BUSH

DUKAKIS

I DON'T KNOW ABOUT YOU, BUT—FRANKLY—I AM BEGINNING TO GET GROSSED OUT!

LINCOLN

DOUGLAS

©1988 THE COMMERCIAL APPEAL

SCOTT STANTIS
Courtesy Memphis Commercial Appeal

48

Berry's World

© 1988 by NEA, Inc. *Jim Berry*

THE SCARLET LETTER — 1988

JIM BERRY
Courtesy NEA

KEVIN KALLAUGHER
Courtesy the Economist

CHRIS OBRION
Courtesy Potomac News

Dear Vice-President Bush,

Hope you are in the pink of health. It *is* the cold and flu season, you know. Stay well!

A concerned American,
Flora Beetlemeyer

Dear Mr. Bush:

Did you know that a well-balanced diet and a program of regular exercise can ensure a long and healthy life?

Just asking.

Ed and Myrtle Johnson

DEAR MR. BUSH:
ENCLOSED IS A GROSS OF VITAMINS.

BEST WISHES,
D. WILLSON

P.S. HOW ADEQUATE IS YOUR SECRET SERVICE PROTECTION?

REFLECTIONS ON THE QUAYLE-BENTSEN DEBATE

POTOMAC NEWS/88

49

VEEP DEBATE

ART HENRIKSON
Courtesy Des Plaines Daily Herald

IF ABRAHAM LINCOLN RAN FOR PRESIDENT TODAY...

ABE, AS YOUR SPIN DOCTOR, I WARN YA— WE CAN'T GET A DECENT SOUND-BITE OUT OF THIS SPEECH!

GETTYSBURG ADDRESS

LINDA BOILEAU
Courtesy Frankfort State Journal

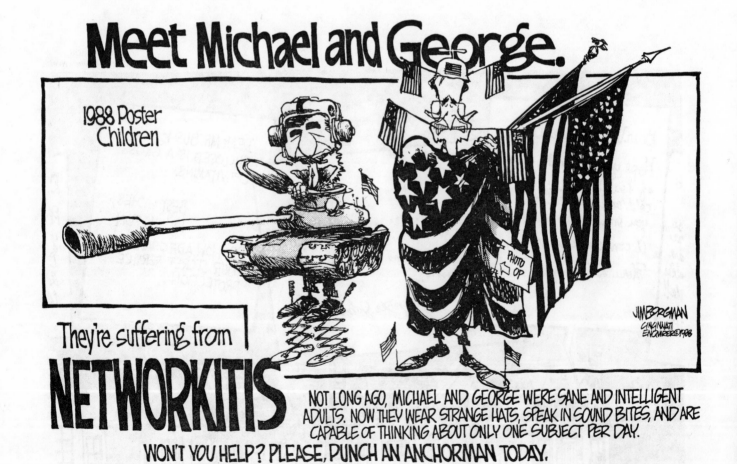

Meet Michael and George.

1988 Poster Children

They're suffering from

NETWORKITIS

NOT LONG AGO, MICHAEL AND GEORGE WERE SANE AND INTELLIGENT ADULTS. NOW THEY WEAR STRANGE HATS, SPEAK IN SOUND BITES, AND ARE CAPABLE OF THINKING ABOUT ONLY ONE SUBJECT PER DAY.

WON'T YOU HELP? PLEASE, PUNCH AN ANCHORMAN TODAY.

JIM BORGMAN
Courtesy Cincinnati Enquirer

50

MIKE JENKINS
Courtesy Springfield (Va.) Journal

CARTOONIST'S DILEMMA

C'MON! VOTE YOUR CONSCIENCE, YOU KNOW WHICH MAN'S THE BEST QUALIFIED FOR THE JOB.

YEH, BUT TH' SHORT GUY WITH TH' BIG NOSE IS REAL EASY TO DRAW... GET OUT AND VOTE!

HANK McCLURE
Courtesy Lawton (Okla.) Constitution

51

WELL__THAT'S IT, GRANDMOTHER__ IT'LL BE **BUSH** VS **DUKAKIS**__

IS THAT BECAUSE OF THE WRITERS' STRIKE?

CLICK

CHARLES DANIEL
Courtesy Knoxville Journal

SCOTT STANTIS
Courtesy Memphis Commercial Appeal

...FINALLY, A PRESIDENTIAL RACE BASED ON ISSUES! COMPLETE WITH SUBSTANTIVE DEBATE!! COMING UP NEXT!!!

CLICK

♪ FLINTSTONES, ♪ MEET THE FLINTSTONES... ♪

52

Live and Learn...

JON KENNEDY
Courtesy Arkansas Democrat

JOHN STAMPONE
Courtesy Salisbury Daily Times

GEORGE DANBY
Courtesy Bangor Daily News

America's Cup
DEFENDER
"STARS & STRIPES"
GEORGE BUSH

CHALLENGER
"SNOW BLOWER"
MIKE DUKAKIS

...SO REMEMBER, STUDENTS, IT'S VERY IMPORTANT TO DEVELOP HIGH MORAL STANDARDS IN ORDER TO BECOME RESPONSIBLE ADULT CITIZENS!

NOW - FOR OUR CURRENT EVENTS ACTIVITY FOR TODAY, CHARLOTTE IS GOING TO READ TODAY'S TOP HEADLINES!

FORMER WHITE HOUSE AIDE CONVICTED OF INFLUENCE-PEDDLING!

ARIZONA GOVERNOR GOES ON TRIAL!

JOE BIDEN PLAGIARIZES!

GARY HART SAYS IT'S NOBODY'S BUSINESS!

ATTORNEY GENERAL UNDER INVESTIGATION!

TOM ADDISON
Courtesy Independent-Mail (S.C.)

TOM CURTIS
Courtesy National Review

SECOND DEBATE

"*Governor, you're no Jack Kennedy.*"

54

Congress

During the first half of 1988, Congress voted to ratify an arms-control treaty with the Soviets, overhaul the federal trade policy, expand Medicare to include catastrophic medical costs, and provide drought relief for American farmers. During the last half of the year, however, Democrats and Republicans failed to solve such issues as federal day-care assistance, defense programs, and the matter of ethics.

Democrats leaned heavily on officials of the Reagan Administration who had been investigated, indicted, or forced from office under a cloud of corruption charges. Republicans, on the other hand, insisted House Speaker Jim Wright (D-Texas) had released classified information in discussing C.I.A. involvement in Nicaragua and that he had used his office for personal enrichment. The House ethics committee finally agreed to take a look at the latter charge.

In June, the House and Senate agreed on a $1.1 trillion fiscal 1989 budget, which included a $135.3 billion deficit. Congress also rejected further military aid to the Contras in Nicaragua.

Many members of Congress continued to call for higher taxes, and a $4 billion package affecting defense contractors and others who sell to the government was approved.

KIRK WALTERS
Courtesy Toledo Blade

POLL SHOWS MOST AMERICANS ARE
IGNORANT ABOUT WORLD GEOGRAPHY

BILL SANDERS
Courtesy Milwaukee Journal

MICHAEL P. RAMIREZ
Courtesy Copley News Service

"Menus, Gentlemen?"

DEMOCRATIC CONGRESS

FIRST THE GOOD NEWS . . . .

MY CONSTITUENTS SAY I HAVE GREAT STATURE IN FISCAL MATTERS

. . . . a BIG $PENDER

ROTHCO

57

WHY DON'T WE DO WHAT WE'VE DONE BEFORE? THROW MONEY AT THE PROBLEM.

DEFICIT REDUCTION

JEFF DANZIGER
Courtesy Christian Science Monitor

THE WRIGHT STUFF
JIM WRIGHT

LAMBERT DER
Courtesy Greenville (S.C.) News

CONGRESSIONAL SIGN·Shop

WARNING! JOGGING MAY CAUSE HARDENING OF THE TOES!

WARNING! LAWYERS MAY BE HAZARDOUS TO YOUR SAVINGS!

PIT BULL! WARNING! THIS DOG MAY BE FATAL TO YOUR HEALTH!

WARNING! CATS CAN CAUSE SCRATCHES!

...RNING!
DEATH IS NOT FUNNY!

WARNING! TOO MUCH TV CAN CAUSE MENTAL ILLNESS.

WARNING! ILLITERACY MAY PREVENT YOU FROM READING THIS!

WARNING! THIS MACHINE EATS FINGERS.

WARNING! FAILURE TO READ WARNING SIGNS CAN LEAD TO STUPIDITY!

CIGARETTES

WARNING! THIS APRON MAY CAUSE YOU TO TRIP!

WARNING! BOOZE

WARNING! BOOZE

WARNING! THIS CARTOON MAY OR MAY NOT BE FUNNY.

JERRY BARNETT
Courtesy Indianapolis News

58

NOTE: STORE NEAR A PORK BARREL

UNCLE JIM'S FLAKEY DEALS

Adds Flavor to Ethics, Book Deals and Central American Issues...

BUBBA FLINT
Courtesy Dallas/Ft. Worth Suburban

AS SPEAKER OF THE HOUSE, I RESENT THESE CALLS TO INVESTIGATE MY FINANCES! WHY ME?? **ALL** POLITICIANS PASS THE HAT!

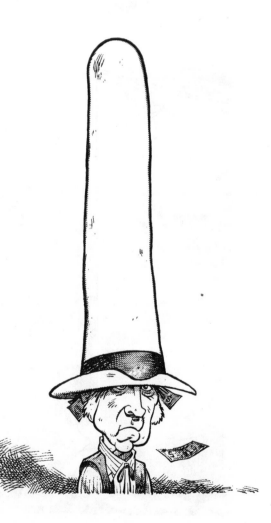

DICK WRIGHT
Courtesy Providence Journal-Bulletin

59

TAKEOVERS

GREAT SCOTT WATKINS, WE JUST ACCIDENTLY TOOK OVER OUR OWN COMPANY!

ACME

SOMEDAY, SON, A TAKEOVER WILL PREVENT ALL THIS FROM BEING YOURS.

The Economy

Following the global stock market crash in October 1987, most financial analysts expected 1988 to bring severe economic problems, perhaps even a depression such as the one that followed the Wall Street collapse of 1929. But such dire predictions were off the mark, and the U.S. economy maintained remarkable strength. Unemployment declined to its lowest level in fourteen years, and the Gross National Product rose more than 3 percent in the first six months of the year.

Corporate mergers continued at a record pace during the year. Eastman Kodak bought Sterling Drug for $5.1 billion, Rupert Murdoch purchased Triangle Publications for $3 billion, and Kraft was grabbed off by Philip Morris, which already owned General Foods. The new company is now the world's largest producer of consumer goods.

In late November, Kohberg, Kravis and Roberts purchased R.J.R. Nabisco for $24.88 billion—the largest takeover in U.S. history.

Japanese firms continued their acquisitions of prime real estate and businesses in the U.S. More than half of the office buildings in downtown Los Angeles are now owned by Japanese companies.

The Christian Science Monitor

JEFF DANZIGER
Courtesy Christian Science Monitor

61

RALPH DUNAGIN
Courtesy Orlando Sentinel

"YOUR HONOR, MAY I REMIND THE COURT THAT MY CLIENTS OWN THIS BUILDING?"

EDGAR SOLLER
Courtesy Daily Breeze

WE'RE HAVING TO CLOSE THE MILL HERE, BUT THE REAGAN PEOPLE TELL US THERE ARE SOME OPENINGS IN JAPAN.... IF YOU CAN BE THERE BY THURSDAY.

EUGENE PAYNE
Courtesy Charlotte Observer

62

THIS IS FANTASTIC! ACCORDING TO THE INTERPRETATION THE MAYA ENGAGED IN SOME SORT OF BUYOUT AND MERGER FRENZY JUST PRIOR TO THEIR VANISHING FROM THE FACE OF THE EARTH.

CRAIG MACINTOSH
Courtesy Minneapolis Star-Tribune

TOO BAD YOU'RE NOT A VICTIM OF INCOMPETENT MANAGEMENT!

CORPORATE BAILOUTS

THE MILWAUKEE JOURNAL

BILL SANDERS
Courtesy Milwaukee Journal

63

LARRY WRIGHT
Courtesy Detroit News

...AND THIS IS THE ADDRESS IN TOKYO WHERE YOU'LL SEND THE MORTGAGE PAYMENTS...

NOT BAD... BUT COULD YOU DO IT TWICE IN A ROW?!!

ROGER SCHILLERSTROM
Courtesy Crain's Chicago Business

JIM BORGMAN
Courtesy Cincinnati Enquirer

THE HOSTILE TAKEOVER

PAUL CONRAD
Courtesy Los Angeles Times

MORNING IN AMERICA

JIM BORGMAN
Courtesy Cincinnati Enquirer

THE SPIKE IS DRIVEN CONNECTING ALL THE MALLS IN AMERICA

65

BOY! LOOK AT ALL THOSE TV CAMERAS DOWN THERE! WHAT DO YOU SUPPOSE THEY'RE FILMING?

THE BLIGHT OF REAGANOMICS!

CHUCK ASAY
Courtesy Colorado Springs
Gazette-Telegraph

SERVE YOURSELF

WE HAVE ENERGY !!!
WHY PUT NUCLEAR PLANTS ON LINE? WE'LL GIVE YOU LINE!

OPEC GAS AND OIL PRICES

SAME OLD OPEC MESSAGE: "HANG IN THERE!"

JIM DOBBINS
Courtesy Manchester Union Leader

66

The Deficit

The debate in Congress over how to cope with the growing budget deficit continued during 1988, remaining one of the nation's major issues through much of the decade.

Under an agreement reached in 1987, Congress and the administration set spending ceilings in advance on domestic needs, defense, and in the international field. Both Democrats and Republicans showed signs of finally becoming serious about dealing with the deficit. Congress consistently has added to the president's proposed budget each year as pork-barrel spending continued.

In June, the Senate and the House agreed on a $1.1 trillion fiscal 1989 budget that reflected a $135.3 billion deficit. This was just under the Gramm-Rudman deficit-reduction law requirement of a maximum deficit of $136 billion.

A vow by President Reagan in his State of the Union address to veto any omnibus bill that combined all government spending in one package helped force the lawmakers to settle their differences. Just before the October 1 deadline, Congress completed its work on all thirteen appropriations bills, the first time since 1976 the target had been met.

PAUL CONRAD
Courtesy Los Angeles Times

DRAWING UP THE WILL

67

—YEH, JUST KEEP IT ON UNTIL AFTER NOVEMBER!

DEFICIT

THE RED SEA

DEFICIT

"NO, IT'S NEVER WORKED BEFORE... BUT AT LEAST YOU FEEL LIKE YOU'RE DOING SOMETHING."

AW HECK SAM, RELAX! WITH ME YOU'RE IN GOOD HANDS

DEFICIT

DEFICIT

It's Mine, All Mine!!

DEFENSE SPENDING AIDS DRUGS ARMS CONTROL ECONOMY ENVIRONMENTAL WASTE

68

HEY! BIG SPENDER!

THE REAGAN DEFICIT

MASS. DEFICIT

FRANK EVERS
Courtesy New York Post

O.O.H SAY CAN YOU SEEEEE

NO! NO! NO! I PLEDGE ALLEGIANCE...

DEFICIT

JACK HIGGINS
Courtesy Chicago Sun-Times

READ MY LIPS

DEFICITS

KEN ALEXANDER
Courtesy Copley News

Ahhh... Now I can Relax

BUSH WINS

Deficit

DOUGLAS REGALIA
Courtesy Contra Costa Sun

MIKE LUCKOVICH
Courtesy New Orleans Times-Picayune

Adios, Ron!

Isn't that gorgeous! Ronald Reagan riding off into the eclipse!...

Deficit

U.S. Defense

Tension in the Persian Gulf increased during 1988, with several hostile confrontations between the U.S. Navy and Iran. In early July, the cruiser *Vincennes,* which was equipped with highly sophisticated Aegis computer-controlled radar and weapons systems, mistook an Iranian airliner for a jet fighter. The crew of the *Vincennes* concluded the jetliner was heading directly for the ship with the intent to attack. The White House apologized for the downing of the plane and said compensation would be paid to the families of those who perished.

The INF (Intermediate-range Nuclear Forces) treaty that had been signed by President Reagan and Russia's Mikhail Gorbachev in 1987 was finally ratified by the U.S. Senate after extensive wrangling.

In June, the U.S. Department of Justice uncovered a massive procurement scandal involving alleged bribery and fraud among defense contractors and a few high-ranking Pentagon officials. It was alleged that some contractors charged the government millions of dollars illegally. One company had to pay $115 million in fines for overcharging.

A computer whiz somehow crippled the Pentagon's Arpanet data network temporarily by use of a computer "virus," a programming procedure that duplicates itself, slowing or shutting down the system's 6,000 computers.

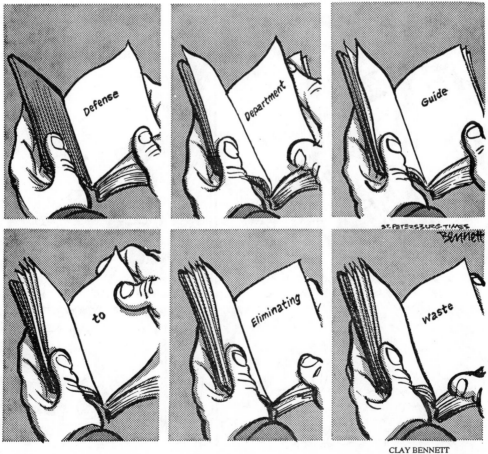

CLAY BENNETT
Courtesy St. Petersburg Times

McDonnell-
Douglas
OVER 250 SUBPOENAS SERVED
BRIBE THRU

Naughty boy! Now you call the president, say you're sorry and promise you won't do it again!

72

DANI AGUILA
Courtesy Filipino Reporter

DEADLY S.P.I.D.E.R. (SCANDAL IN THE PENTAGON INVOLVING DEFENSE EMPLOYEES RECREANT)

EDDIE GERMANO
Courtesy Brockton Enterprise

DUKAKIS SAYS HE WOULD RELY ON THE COOPERATION OF OUR ALLIES IN CASES OF POTENTIAL INTERNATIONAL THREATS... NEWS

OK FRIENDS... CHARGE !

THE DUKE ISN'T UP ON PAST HISTORY

DOUG MACGREGOR
Courtesy Norwich Bulletin

SUPER POWER TOY STORE

PENTAGON BUDGET BUSTERS

WHAT DO YOU MEAN I CAN'T HAVE 600 SHIPS ?!!! "CAP" GOT JOHNNY LEHMAN 600 SHIPS! NOW, I WANT 600 SHIPS, I NEED 600 SHIPS, AND IF YOU DON'T BUY ME 600 SHIPS, I QUIT!!

LITTLE JIMMY WEBB MAKES A SCENE...

73

"I PLEDGE ALLEGIANCE..."

INSIDER TRADING IS DISGUSTING!

IT'S DAMAGED WALL STREET'S CREDIBILITY!

YEAH! THEM, TOO!

The Mideast

The Palestinian uprising which began in 1987 in the occupied West Bank gained momentum in 1988 as Arabs vented their frustration over twenty years of Israeli rule. Arab teenagers threw rocks and sometimes gasoline bombs at Israeli soldiers, who retaliated with bullets, beatings, tear gas, bulldozing of homes, and deportations of suspected leaders. By the end of 1988, some three hundred Palestinians had been killed, and much of Israel's good will around the world had eroded.

In July, King Hussein of Jordan announced that he would cut all formal ties with the West Bank, which left the Palestine Liberation Organization with the problem of paying the salaries of governmental officials and for administrative services in the region.

The November election in Israel resulted in a virtual dead heat between the Likud, headed by Prime Minister Yitzhak Shamir, and the Labor Party. Shamir appeared to retain his post through a shaky coalition.

The years-old Iran-Iraq war officially ended on August 20, and direct talks between the two combatants began in Geneva. By year's end, however, no official settlement had been reached.

RAY OSRIN
Courtesy Cleveland Plain Dealer

BEATING PALESTINIANS
INTO PLOWSHARES

JOSH BEUTEL
Courtesy Telegraph-Journal (New Bruns.)

GARY MARKSTEIN
Courtesy Tribune Newspapers

PALESTINIAN PROTESTERS

OCCUPIED LAND

76

STEVE SACK
Courtesy Minneapolis Star-Tribune

THE BEATINGS CONTINUE....

Berry's World

THE IRANIAN TAR BABY

JIM BERRY
Courtesy NEA

WHO WON? NO ONE.

IRAN-IRAQ WAR

BRIAN DUFFY
Courtesy Des Moines Register

I FIRED A SHOT INTO THE AIR— IT FELL TO EARTH I KNOW NOT WHERE

ISRAEL

DRAPER HILL
Courtesy Detroit News

77

FIRST IMPRESSIONS COUNT:
1. RECOGNIZE ISRAEL
2. SHAVE
3. BUY A SUIT

HOW TO FORM A GOVERNMENT

DICK WALLMEYER
Courtesy Long Beach Press-Telegram

M. D. SHELTON
Courtesy Orange County Register

WHILE I'M OUT BLOWING UP WOMEN AND CHILDREN YOU TAKE ON THE ISRAELI ARMY!

PLO

WE MUST MAKE SURE THAT THIS NEVER HAPPENS AGAIN...

AT LEAST NOT TO US...

S. C. RAWLS
Courtesy NEA

BILL SCHORR
Courtesy Kansas City Star

1988 K.C. STAR-LATS
APOLOGIES TO KETCHUM

"WE CAUGHT HIM THROWING STONES...SO WE'RE GONNA BULLDOZE YOUR HOUSE..."

79

KATE SALLEY PALMER
Courtesy Associated Features

MIKE KEEFE
Courtesy Denver Post

OCCUPIED TERRITORIES

life with robinson

JERRY ROBINSON
Courtesy Cartoonists and Writers Syndicate

80

HY ROSEN
Courtesy Albany Times-Union

COPYRIGHT 1988
ALBANY TIMES UNION

"MAYBE HE WAS TRYING TO SWIM FOR IT"
ABBAS COMMENT ON KLINGHOFFER'S BEING SHOT AND PUSHED OVERBOARD

PLO LUV BOAT

ABUL ABBAS

FROM THE BOYS WHO GAVE YOU THE ACHILLE LAURO EPISODE

ISRAEL? WHAT ISRAEL?

ISRAEL? WHAT ISRAEL?

ISRAEL? WHAT ISRAEL?

ISRAEL? WHAT ISRAEL?

UM... ISRAEL?

YOU DID IT!

AFTER 40 YEARS OF DENIAL — FINALLY THE PLO HAS RECOGNIZED YOU!

PLO? WHAT PLO?

SHAMIR

JOHN TREVER
Courtesy Albuquerque Journal

MARK CULLUM
Courtesy Birmingham News

CEASE FIRE!

IRAN

PAUL SZEP
Courtesy Boston Globe

I'VE BEEN TOO KIND... FOR TOO LONG!

THE AYADOLLAH

So alright already! We recognize the Jews!

So maybe we don't!

ISRAELI TIMES

'WHO IS A JEW' LAW FORCED BY ULTRA-ORTHODOX PARTIES

THREE-QUARTERS OF ISRAELI POPULATION MAY NOT BE KOSHER

ROY PETERSON
Courtesy Vancouver Sun

WHAT IS THIS THING? OF WHAT USE IS IT?!? IT DOESN'T APPEAR TO HAVE A DETONATOR..! ..OR EVEN A TRIGGER.!...

PLO · Diplomacy

CLYDE WELLS
Courtesy Augusta Chronicle

DAVE GRANLUND
Courtesy Middlesex (Mass.) News

NO RIFFRAFF!

UN BAR & GRILLE

BOUNCER

ARAFAT

NOAH BEE
Courtesy J.T.A. Syndicate

JIMMY MARGULIES
Courtesy Houston Post

STEVE GREENBERG
Courtesy Seattle Post-Intelligencer

84

Russia

By 1988, "glasnost," a policy of more openness first announced by Communist Party leader Mikhail Gorbachev in 1986, was encouraging opponents of Soviet restrictions to speak out. There were outbreaks of violence between ethnic minorities, something new to Russia, and intellectuals expressed controversial views more openly. Corruption during Leonid Brezhnev's rule was disclosed, and his son-in-law was put on trial for bribery.

Soviet troops began withdrawing from Afghanistan as Gorbachev had promised, but in November the withdrawal was halted and military activity increased when the Soviets charged that Pakistan was still supplying U.S. arms to the rebel forces.

Gorbachev visited New York in December to meet with President Reagan and to address the United Nations but cut his visit short when a massive earthquake struck Soviet Armenia, killing tens of thousands.

Andrei Gromyko, a member of the Soviets' "old guard" who had been a power for almost half a century, resigned from the Politburo and as chairman of the Presidium of the Supreme Soviet. Several other holdovers from other eras also retired, adding to the new look of the Soviet Union.

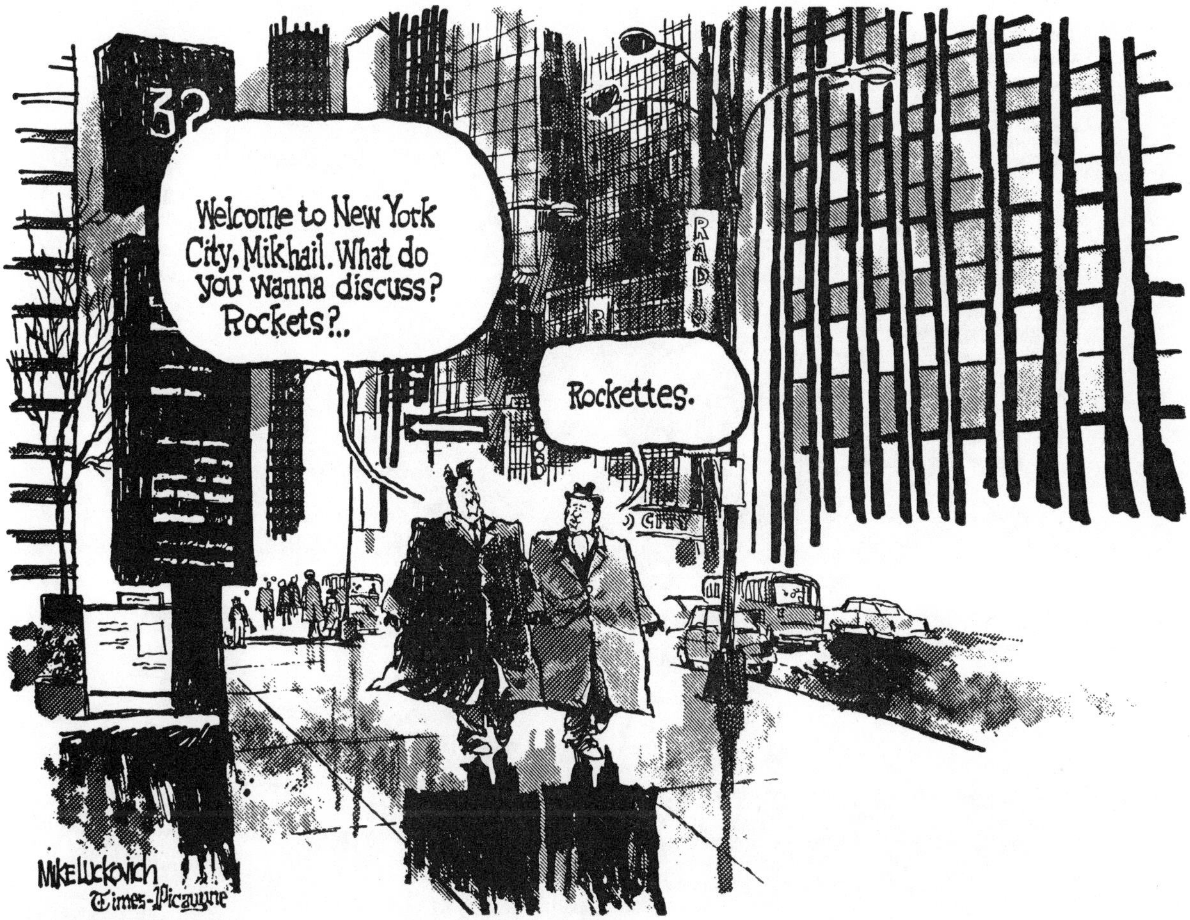
Welcome to New York City, Mikhail. What do you wanna discuss? Rockets?..
Rockettes.
RADIO
MIKE LUCKOVICH Times-Picayune

MIKE LUCKOVICH
Courtesy New Orleans Times-Picayune

TOM ENGELHARDT
Courtesy St. Louis Post-Dispatch

ETTA HULME
Courtesy Ft. Worth Star-Telegram

'I Try Loosening Up, Doc, And The Aches And Pains
Just Seem To Get Worse'

JOHN DEERING
Courtesy Arkansas Democrat

86

CLOSET KEEP CLOSED

Human Rights

RON, STAY WITH THE GROUP!!

Soviet Open House TOUR

Gorby

MIKE LUCKOVICH
Courtesy New Orleans Times-Picayune

GENE BASSET
Courtesy Atlanta Journal

RIP

OLD GUARD

PERESTROIKA

87

MILT PRIGGEE
Courtesy Spokane Spokesman-Review

"DUE TO PERESTROIKA ALL HISTORY TESTS HAVE BEEN POSTPONED UNTIL WE KNOW WHAT THE NEW FACTS OF HISTORY ARE..."

DICK WRIGHT
Courtesy Providence Journal-Bulletin

I'VE GOT GOOD NEWS! WE'VE GOT A PULL-OUT DATE!

AFGHANISTAN

OFF THE SOVIET PIGS!

TELL THE COMRADE FROM ESTONIA I'D LIKE A WORD WITH HIM...

© 1988 SCRIPPS HOWARD UNITED FEATURE SYND.

HENRY PAYNE
Courtesy Scripps Howard News Service

OUR MINORITIES ARE RIOTING... OUR YOUTH ARE DISENCHANTED... OUR INVOLVEMENT IN AFGHANISTAN IS A FIASCO... WHAT NEXT, COMRADE, WHAT NEXT?

SOVIET WOMEN UNITE!

YOU'VE COME A LONG WAY, BABUSHKA

PRAVDA

ARMENIA

89

JERRY FEARING
Courtesy St. Paul Pioneer Press-Dispatch

MARK CULLUM
Courtesy Birmingham News

JEFF STAHLER
Courtesy Cincinnati Post

90

Central America

The regional peace plan signed in 1987 by five Central American presidents seeking a peaceful settlement between Nicaragua's Sandinista government and the Contras went up in smoke during the year. The six-year-old war to topple the Nicaraguan government appeared to have been lost as more than eleven thousand Contra freedom fighters retreated to camps in Honduras and were followed by hundreds of civilian supporters. Contra officials admitted they could no longer muster any real resistance without full resumption of U.S. aid, which had been cut off by Congress.

In Panama, political and economic turmoil grew as strongman General Manuel Noriega thwarted U.S. efforts to oust him. Reports linked Noriega to the cocaine trade, and in February he was indicted by federal grand juries in Florida on drug charges.

In Cuba, Fidel Castro defended Leninist orthodoxy and announced that his country would not follow Russia's lead of reforming its economic and political system. On the whole, the Cuban people seemed worse off in 1988.

Hurricane Gilbert devastated Jamaica in September, with 115-mile-per-hour winds causing 36 deaths and leaving 500,000 people homeless. In October, Hurricane Joan roared through Nicaragua, killing scores and wrecking the homes of 300,000.

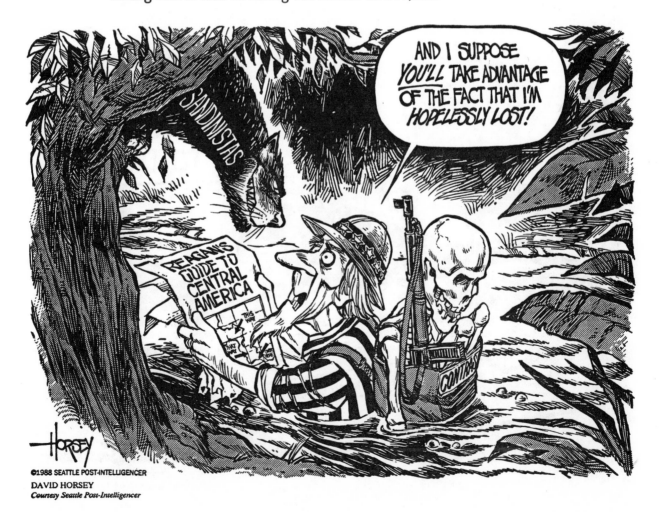

©1988 SEATTLE POST-INTELLIGENCER
DAVID HORSEY
Courtesy Seattle Post-Intelligencer

91

JOHN TREVER
Courtesy Albuquerque Journal

JUST SAY **NO**RIEGA TO DRUGS

STEVE GREENBERG
Courtesy Seattle Post-Intelligencer

Berry's World

ANOTHER SANDINISTA VICTIM

JIM BERRY
Courtesy NEA

CASH? WHAT PROBLEM?

AISLIN
Courtesy Montreal Gazette

BOB GORRELL
Courtesy Richmond News-Leader

IS HE OUT, YET?...

PANAMA

NORIEGA

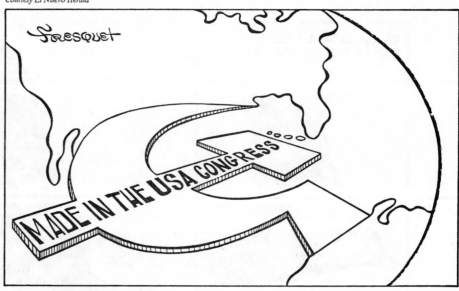

THE BIG SQUEEZE CONTINUES!

94

STEVE KELLEY
Courtesy San Diego Union

BEN SARGENT
Courtesy Austin American-Statesman

HANK MCCLURE
Courtesy Lawton (Okla.) Constitution

NOW...

AISLIN
Courtesy Montreal Gazette

JACK HIGGINS
Courtesy Chicago Sun-Times

NEVER CRY FREEDOM IN A CROWDED THEATRE ...

Foreign Affairs

The government of Haiti played musical chairs again during the year. Early in 1988, the military regime of General Henri Namphy was replaced by a civilian group headed by Leslie Manigat, but in June Namphy regained power through a coup. Then, in September, Namphy again was forced out. Haiti remains the hemisphere's poorest country, with primitive farming methods and a stagnant economy.

Strikes and political dissension created more turmoil in Poland. A 40 percent increase in food prices led to the reemergence of the outlawed labor union Solidarity. As strikes spread, the government resigned and was replaced by a more orthodox communist regime which agreed to talks with Solidarity representatives.

In Ethiopia, where 7 million people were facing death from starvation, the government turned the distribution of relief supplies into a political tool. All foreign relief agencies and workers were ordered to channel distribution through governmental agencies.

South Africa continued to struggle during the year, with large numbers of whites deserting the ruling Nationalist Party for the right-wing Conservative Party. Austrian President Kurt Waldheim's checkered past continued to draw close scrutiny, and a commission of seven historians cleared him of war crimes but concluded that he had knowledge of war-time atrocities.

EDGAR SOLLER
Courtesy California Examiner

MEN OF THE CROSS

LEN BOROZINSKI
Courtesy Phoenix Gazette

Workers of the World, unite! You have nothing to lose but your chains!
KARL MARX

POLISH COMMUNIST PARTY

JEFF DANZIGER
Courtesy Christian Science Monitor

THE AUSTRIAN DOWNHILL EVENT

BLAINE
Courtesy The Spectator (Ont.)

JERRY BUCKLEY
Courtesy Marybeth Cartoons

STEVEN TURTIL
Courtesy Charleston Daily Mail

99

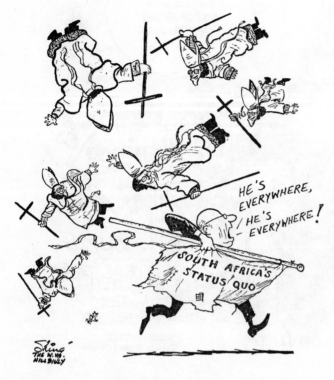

HE'S EVERYWHERE, HE'S EVERYWHERE!

SOUTH AFRICA'S STATUS QUO

BOTHA'S TUTU

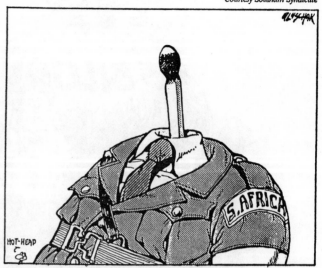

HOT-HEAD

S. AFRICA

SO.... WHAT HAPPENS NEXT?

CHUCK AND DIG

life with robinson

THE COMMISSION SAID I KNEW ABOUT NAZI CRIMES BUT DIDN'T DO ANYTHING ABOUT IT! THAT'S NOT TRUE! I DID DO SOMETHING!...

...I LIED ABOUT IT!

Canadian Affairs

Free trade with the U.S. was the main issue in a hard-fought campaign that saw Canada's Brian Mulroney remain as prime minister. The Conservative victory was a keen disappointment to Liberal leader John Turner, who had forced the election by blocking a free trade treaty in the Canadian senate.

The trade agreement, covering some $200 billion in various trade measures, would have phased out cross-border tariffs by 1998 and guaranteed equal treatment for U.S. and Canadian companies in the two respective countries. Proponents argued that free trade would create badly needed jobs, while critics played on old Canadian fears that the powerful neighbor to the south would economically overpower their country.

Economic growth continued its six-year expansion with a predicted 4 percent rise in the Gross National Product, second only to Japan among major industrialized democracies.

Acid rain continued as a major problem between the U.S. and Canada, and a twenty-five-nation agreement pledged to control pollution from nitrogen oxides beginning at the end of 1994. Bilingualism also remained a heated issue during the year.

EDD ULUSCHAK
Courtesy Southam Syndicate

JOSH BEUTEL
Courtesy Telegraph-Journal (New Bruns.)

...AND I'M SURE THAT NOW I CAN BE BOTH A MINISTER AND GAY... IT WILL NOT INFLUENCE THE SIZE OF OUR CONGREGATION...

DICK GIBSON
Courtesy Toronto Su

FLOW
MADE IN USA

BORDER

JAMES TODD
Courtesy Southam Syndicate

102

BREAKING THE SOUND BARRIER

ART WOOD
Courtesy Farm Bureau News

...AND IF ANYONE KNOWS ANY JUST CAUSE WHY....!

M. R. TINGLEY
Courtesy Ting Cartoons

BRIAN GABLE
Courtesy Toronto Globe and Mail

LEAP OF FAITH

MARGULIES
©1988 HOUSTON POST

Cigarettes
$7.50 PER PACK
INCLUDES
10¢ STATE & 40¢ FED. TAX
$6.00 LEGAL DEFENSE FUND

STAYSKAL
88 TAMPA TRIBUNE

PRISON OVERCROWDING

"I'M SENTENCING YOU TO 25 YEARS IN PRISON WITH NO HOPE OF PAROLE UNTIL AFTER 3 P.M. TOMORROW AFTERNOON!"

Crime and the Courts

The U.S. Supreme Court began to assume a Reagan look during 1988 with the appointment of Anthony Kennedy to replace Lewis Powell, Jr. Kennedy joined two other Reagan appointees, Sandra Day O'Connor and Antonin Scalia, on the conservative-leaning court.

The Justices voted in May that American citizens do not have an "expectation of privacy" when it comes to their garbage. The ruling reversed California courts that had found that police violated Fourth Amendment privacy protections when they searched garbage for clues to crimes.

In a free-speech ruling, the Court decreed that *Hustler* magazine publisher Larry Flynt did not have to pay damages to evangelist Jerry Falwell for a cartoon that portrayed Falwell as a drunkard. The finding overturned a $200,000 damage award previously granted to the evangelist.

Drug-trafficking and gang-related violence rose across the nation. At least 177 gang-related deaths were reported in Los Angeles during the first half of 1988, and Washington, D.C., broke its one-year record of 287 homicides. A Justice Department report revealed that three out of every four men arrested for serious crimes used drugs.

GILL FOX
Courtesy Westport News

105

DON LANDGREN
Courtesy Worcester Sunday Telegram

DICK GIBSON
Courtesy Toronto Sun

DON'T YELL AT ME. THE SUPREME COURT SAID THIS ISN'T YOURS ANYMORE.

LET SOME PUNK TRY AND SNATCH MY PURSE... IT'LL MAKE MY DAY!

FLORIDA RESIDENTS FIND LOOPHOLE IN GUN LAW.

DAVID HORSEY
Courtesy Seattle Post-Intelligencer

Hostage Taking...

MINORITY COMMUNITIES

DRUG GANGS

106

JOEL PETT
Courtesy Lexington (Ky.) Herald-Leader

DRAPER HILL
Courtesy Detroit News

MICHAEL KONOPACKI
Courtesy Huck/Konopacki Labor Cartoons

GOOD MORNING CLASS. I'M SUPREME COURT JUSTICE BYRON WHITE. TODAY WE ARE GOING TO PRACTICE YOUR NEW FIRST AMENDMENT RIGHTS. LET'S BEGIN!

VERY GOOD. NOW, REPEAT AFTER ME, "AMERICA IS THE WORLD'S GREATEST DEMOCRACY"!

107

DAVID O'KEEFE
Courtesy Tampa Tribune

CONVENIENCE STORE NIGHT CLERK

DAVID O'KEEFE
Courtesy Tampa Tribune

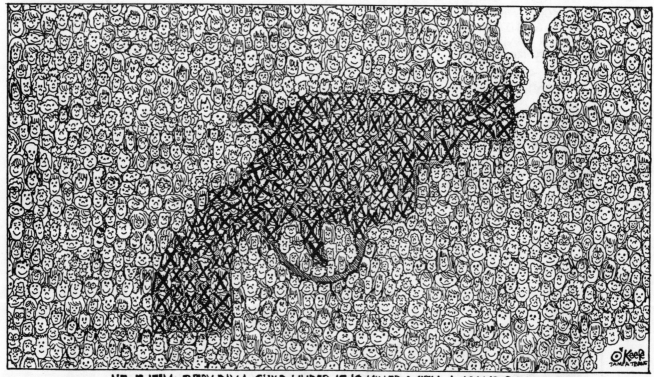

NEWS ITEM: EVERY DAY A CHILD UNDER 15 IS KILLED WITH A HANDGUN.

Health Issues

The threat of AIDS continued to grow at an accelerated pace worldwide during the year. The U.S. Public Health Service estimated that by the end of 1992 some 380,000 people will have contracted the usually fatal disease. The World Health Organization counted more than 96,000 cases of AIDS in 136 countries but estimated that less than half of all cases are officially reported.

Surgeon General C. Everett Koop blanketed the U.S. with information and warnings about AIDS in a brochure mailed to 107 million homes. Research on the disease continued, and AIDS experts from 125 countries met in Stockholm for the fourth International Conference on AIDS.

The anti-abortion movement grew around the country as mass demonstrations were held in many cities, and abortion clinics were picketed.

In an effort to combat a growing drug problem, Congress passed a $2.8 billion bill that also permitted the death penalty for drug-related murders. Constraints of the Gramm-Rudman Law governing spending allowed only $500 million of the approved funds actually to be appropriated.

THE SEXUAL REVOLUTION: UPDATE!

CLYDE WELLS
Courtesy Augusta Chronicle

M. R. TINGLEY
Courtesy Ting Cartoons

RANDY BISH
Courtesy Tribune-Review (Pa.)

THE CORNER STORE OF TOMORROW?
— NOT THE MOM AN' POP VARIETY

ABSTINENCE? THEY HAVENT TOLD US ABOUT SEX YET!

JACK JURDEN
Courtesy Wilmington News-Journal

DON'T GET SICK!

110

ROB ROGERS
Courtesy Pittsburgh Press

© 1988 THE PITTSBURGH PRESS
UNITED FEATURE SYNDICATE

I'M SORRY BUT THAT OVERHEAD COMPARTMENT IS OCCUPIED... MY HUSBAND IS HAVING A CIGARETTE.

BRIAN GABLE
Courtesy Toronto Globe and Mail

WAR ON DRUGS

SPIRIT OF '83

111

SCHOOL "HEALTH" CLINIC

CONDOMS • CONTRACEPTIVES
ABORTION REFERRALS

JUST SAY YES

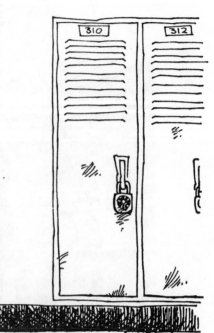

310   312

WE NEED BILLION$

AIDS DEATHS TO REACH 1 MILLION IN THE NEXT TWO YEARS

"THE LIBERAL"

YYAWNNN

FOR 10TH YEAR ABORTION DEATHS WERE OVER 1 MILLION IN 1987

THE SAME "LIBERAL"

DOBBINS
THE UNION LEADER

Doctor, the patient is waking up and we haven't finished the procedure — should we show him the bill again?

CATROW ©1988 HEALTH WEEK Copley News Service

DAVID CATROW
Courtesy Springfield (O.) News-Sun

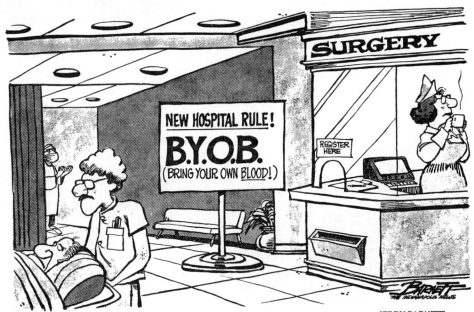

NEW HOSPITAL RULE!
B.Y.O.B.
(BRING YOUR OWN BLOOD!)

SURGERY

REGISTER HERE

BARNETT
THE INDIANAPOLIS NEWS

JERRY BARNETT
Courtesy Indianapolis News

CHARLES BISSELL
Courtesy The Tennessean

SURGEON GENERAL'S WARNING ABOUT 'GOOD EATIN''

"POOR WRETCH! ANOTHER OF LIFE'S LITTLE DEADLY INDULGENCES FLIES THE KOOP"

113

THAT WAS THE SURGEON GENERAL, ED...THERE MAY BE A PROBLEM WITH OUR BIG PORNO BUST...

JOHN BRANCH
Courtesy San Antonio Express-News

A NATURAL CONSEQUENCE OF THE WAR ON DRUGS...

WE HAD TO DESTROY THE CASUAL USERS IN ORDER TO SAVE THEM...

DENNIS DRAUGHON
Courtesy Raleigh Times

114

THE GOOD NEWS

MEDICAL SCIENCE CAN EXTEND YOUR LIFE AN EXTRA 10 YEARS!

—OR IS IT ???

TO DO WHAT, DOC?

SUNSET NURSING HOME

Activities Chart:

BINGO TUES

Geriatrics dilemma

JON KENNEDY
Courtesy Arkansas Democrat

REMEMBER...
NO OVEREATING,
NO ALCOHOL,
NO CIGARETTES,
NO SEX,
NO SWEETS,
NO BETWEEN MEAL SNACKS,
NO FUN,
NO NOTHIN'...

EDNA, BRING ME THE FLYSWATTER.

KIRK WALTERS
Courtesy Toledo Blade

115

BUCK JONES
Courtesy Mason City Globe-Gazette

MIKE ANGELO
Courtesy Main Line Times (Pa.)

The Homeless

President Reagan signed a bill in October that renewed federal assistance to the homeless across the U.S. The bill budgeted some $634 million for 1989 and $683 million for 1990 to be used for emergency food and shelter, job training, education, health care, and other needs of the less fortunate. Since Congress budgeted only $378 million for the program for 1989, however, additional funding will be required in order to fully finance the program.

As more and more media attention was focused on the plight of the homeless during the year, more and more cities launched assistance programs, and many churches and civic groups increased their efforts to help.

DENNIS DRAUGHON
Courtesy Raleigh Times

THE HORN OF PLENTY

BRIAN DUFFY
Courtesy Des Moines Register

VIC CANTONE
Courtesy Rothco

MIKE PETERS
Courtesy Dayton Daily News

A THOUSAND POINTS OF LIGHT,,,,,,,,

OH! SAY DOES THAT STAR-BANGLED BANNER STILL WAVE O'ER THE LAND OF THE FREE AND THE HOME OF THE BRAVE?

MICHAEL KONOPACKI
Courtesy BC&T News

GRANDFATHER, AS THE FIRST AMERICANS, WE FOUGHT TO PROTECT OUR LAND AND LOST. WHY DOES THE GOVERNMENT GIVE MILLIONS OF DOLLARS TO HELP FOREIGNERS FIGHT FOR FREEDOM—AND FORGET NEEDY AMERICANS?

JERRY BUCKLEY
Courtesy Marybeth Cartoons

EDGAR SOLLER
Courtesy California Examiner

119

STEVE LINDSTROM
Courtesy Duluth News-Tribune

Yellow Leaves 39¢ doz. Dry Stalks 3/$1 Parched Seed 59¢ lb. Baked Clay

© 1988 SPENCER NEWSPAPERS

FEDERAL DROUGHT AID

THAT'S IT?

NEIL GRAHAME
Courtesy Creative Graphics

The Drought

A severe drought that many compared to the Dust Bowl period of the 1930s gripped much of the U.S. during 1988. The mighty Mississippi River fell 10.7 feet below the record low-water mark set in 1872 and created havoc with barge shipping. Lake Michigan's level dropped three feet, and many prairie wetlands in the western U.S. dried up.

The drought especially hurt agriculture, not only in the U.S. but around the world. It was estimated that U.S. grain crops would be down 30 percent for 1988. Farm output also was drastically reduced in Canada, Russia, Eastern Europe, and China.

Because of its effect on food production and the farm economy around the globe, the 1988 drought was expected to yield serious consequences for the next three years.

The drought also contributed to one of the worst forest fires in history. More than half of Yellowstone National Park was gutted by fires during the summer—a total loss of more than one million acres. Mount Rushmore National Memorial also was threatened by a 16,000-acre brush fire in South Dakota.

BOB JORGENSEN
Courtesy Midwest Features Syndicate

American Gothic '88

...AND PLEASE... MAKE IT RAIN..

FARM LOSSES

Bender/The Jackson Sun 1988

GREGG BENDER
Courtesy Jackson (Tenn.) Sun

DOUG MACGREGOR
Courtesy Norwich Bulletin

JOE HELLER
Courtesy Green Bay Press-Gazette

"IT'S BEEN SO DRY HARRY DECIDED TO GO OUT AND BUY MORE APPROPRIATE LAWN ORNAMENTS."

122

LOOKS LIKE YOUR GRASS COULD USE SOME RAIN...

IT'S CORN.

I HEAR THE PRESIDENT'S FORMED A TASK FORCE TO STUDY THE EFFECTS OF THE DROUGHT ON AGRICULTURE.

I HOPE IT AIN'T THE SAME BUNCH STUDYIN' ACID RAIN.

123

Environmental Protection Agency — enforcement division, speaking.

TOM DARCY
Courtesy Newsday

VIC HARVILLE
Courtesy Arkansas Democrat

WELCOME TO SUNSHINE BEACH NEW JERSEY'S FINEST

The Environment

Early in the year an international panel of scientists released a report, sponsored by NASA, declaring that stratospheric ozone was being deleted over the northern hemisphere. Such loss had been noted before over the Antarctic, and there were signs an ozone hole was forming over the Arctic.

Summer swimmers in the Long Island area were ordered off beaches when garbage and medical and hospital wastes began washing ashore. In October, Congress passed a law making it a federal crime to dump medical wastes into the ocean.

Hazardous wastes continued to be hauled across the country, and the Environmental Protection Agency was criticized for moving too slowly in making the responsible companies clean up the dumps they had created. Pressed by congressional deadlines, the EPA ordered that hundreds of chemicals must be made nonhazardous before they could be dumped in landfills.

The U.S. Public Health Service announced that the threat of lung cancer from exposure to radon is greater than had been previously believed. Radon is a colorless, odorless, radioactive gas that occurs naturally in some types of soil and can accumulate under or in homes.

V. CULLUM ROGERS
Courtesy Durham Morning Herald

JACK JURDEN
Courtesy Wilmington News-Journal

DON'T YOU THINK YOU'RE CARRYING THIS RADON GAS THING TOO FAR ?.

BRIAN GABLE
Courtesy Toronto Globe and Mail

BRUCE BEATTIE
Courtesy Daytona Beach News-Journal

"You know, Harriet, maybe it's time we worried about the 'greenhouse effect'... "

126

CHUCK ASAY
*Courtesy Colorado Springs
Gazette-Telegraph*

JOHN TREVER
Courtesy Albuquerque Journal

"OF COURSE WE HAVE A POLICY OF PUTTING OUT FIRES! WE JUST PREFER TO DO IT NATURE'S WAY...."

127

RANDY WICKS
Courtesy Newhall (Calif.) Signal

WHICH OF THESE MAMMALS IS MORE INTELLIGENT?

RANDY WICKS
Courtesy Newhall (Calif.) Signal

ED WAS A REGULAR GUY.

ED WORRIED ABOUT THE GREENHOUSE EFFECT. ABOUT THE OZONE LAYER.

COUGH COUGH

AND ABOUT FOULED BEACHES. AND PESTICIDES IN FOOD.

THE WORLD WAS TOO DANGEROUS, ED DECIDED.

527

SO HE NEVER WENT OUT AGAIN. ED STAYED IN HIS HOME.

AND THE RADON GOT HIM.

STUART CARLSON
Courtesy Milwaukee Sentinel

DAN SHEFELMAN
Courtesy New York Newsday

SO YOU THINK THIS PLANET CAN SUSTAIN INTELLIGENT LIFE?

SURE! THE QUESTION IS, CAN INTELLIGENT LIFE SUSTAIN THIS PLANET...

BEACH CLOSED

POLLUTERS' WORLD NO HUMANS LEFT!

ENVIRONMENTALISTS' WORLD NO HUMANS ALLOWED!

WHY CAN'T WE HAVE A HAPPY MEDIUM?

JERRY BARNETT
Courtesy Indianapolis News

129

YOU'RE SAFE AND SOUND IN YOUR OWN BED, IN YOUR OWN ROOM, IN YOUR OWN HOUSE WITH RADON GAS IN THE BASEMENT, LEAD IN THE WATER PIPES, FORMALDEHYDE IN ITS CONSTRUCTION MATERIALS AND DEADLY TOXINS IN HOUSEHOLD CLEANERS AND PESTICIDES STORED IN THE KITCHEN. SO RELAX AND GO TO SLEEP.

BOB RICH
Courtesy New Haven Register

"FOR THE BEAUTY OF THE EARTH, FOR THE GLORY OF THE SKIES..."

M. R. TINGLEY
Courtesy Ting Cartoons

WELL, WE HAVE FISH WITH ACID RAIN, FISH WITH INDUSTRIAL WASTE OR JUST FISH WITH ORDINARY POLLUTANTS....

AL LIEDERMAN
Courtesy Rothco

130

LINDA BOILEAU
Courtesy Frankfort State Journal

...Here I am, stranded on an island in the middle of nowhere...

...Nothing to remind me of home but the stray plastic six-pack holders, garbage bags, hypodermic needles, styrofoam cups, sewage and contaminated fish that wash up on my little beach...

SCOTT WILLIS
Courtesy San Jose Mercury-News

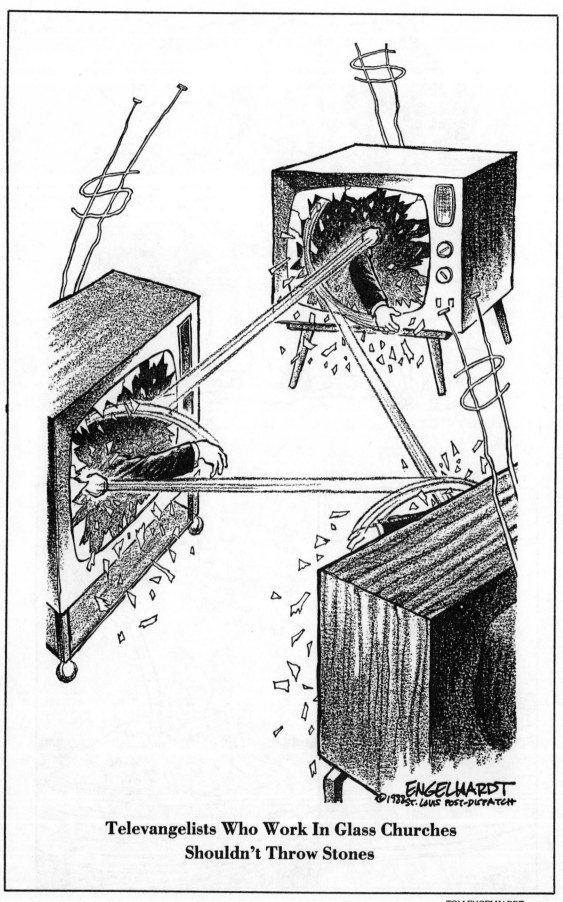

ENGELHARDT
©1988 St. Louis Post-Dispatch

Televangelists Who Work In Glass Churches Shouldn't Throw Stones

TOM ENGELHARDT
Courtesy St. Louis Post-Dispatch

Religion

The Last Temptation of Christ, a movie released in 1988 based on the novel by Nikos Kazantzakis, set off demonstrations and protests from religious groups and churchgoers because it presented Jesus Christ as being tempted by human pleasures and struggling to avoid his death on the cross. Many cities banned the film, and reviews were mixed—some contending it was poorly done and blasphemous, others maintaining it was a masterpiece that showed a human side of the Son of God.

Defrocked evangelist Jim Bakker, who admitted to having sexual relations with a former church secretary in 1987, sought to regain control of the debt-ridden PTL organization. He made a bid of some $175 million to regain the organization he headed before the scandal, but he was unable to show sufficient cash or credit to support the bid. A federal bankruptcy judge ordered Bakker and his wife Tammy and former aide David Taggart to repay $7.7 million to the PTL for mismanagement.

Jimmy Swaggart, another defrocked television evangelist, returned to the pulpit in May, but his TV ministry faced a huge drop in contributions and many stations canceled his programs.

In September, Pope John Paul II defined the female role in terms of motherhood and the home, essentially rejecting wider responsibilities for women.

THE LAST TEMPTATION OF GOD

SPYDER WEBB
Courtesy Blade-Tribune

133

THE LOAD GETS HEAVIER

EDDIE GERMANO
Courtesy Brockton Enterprise

LOU BLOSS
*Courtesy Alexandria (La.) Daily
Town Talk*

134

NOW
PLAYING
MARTIN
SCORSESE'S
"THE LAST
TEMPTATION
OF CHRIST"
A UNIVERSAL
RELEASE

GILL FOX
Courtesy Westport News

FRED MULHEARN
Courtesy Baton Rouge Morning Advocate

EUGENE PAYNE
Courtesy Charlotte Observer

J. D. CROWE
Courtesy San Diego Tribune

CHRIS OBRION
Courtesy Potomac News

136

Space / Air Travel

The U.S. space program regained momentum in late September with the successful launching of the shuttle Discovery. It had been nearly three years since the Challenger tragedy, and the Soviet Union had pulled ahead of the U.S. in almost every area of space exploration. The European Space Agency achieved five successful launches, and the Japanese began developing their own space shuttle.

Airline passenger traffic almost equaled that of 1987, a record year, but not all was roses within the industry. Eastern Airlines was embroiled in a labor-management struggle, dismissing some four thousand employees in an effort to streamline operations, and concern about air safety weighed heavily on every airline.

The most bizarre incident occurred over Hawaii when an eighteen-foot section of the fuselage of a Boeing 737 tore away, killing a flight attendant. The pilot, however, was able to land safely. The plane had been in service for nineteen years, and the accident prompted airlines to inspect carefully older aircraft for cracks and metal fatigue.

The FAA ordered cutbacks in peak-hour landings at O'Hare Airport, the nation's busiest, in Chicago after a series of mistakes in air traffic control.

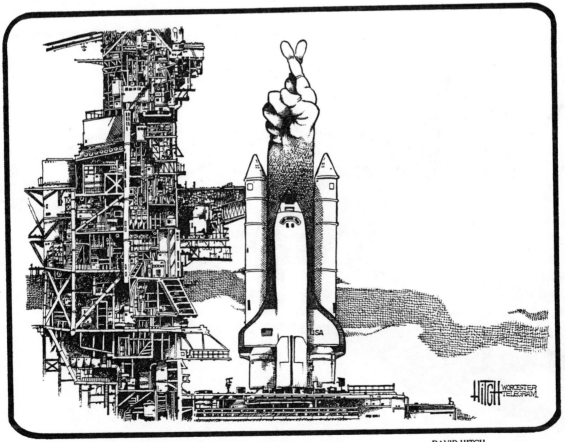

DAVID HITCH
Courtesy Worcester Telegram-Gazette

JERRY FEARING
Courtesy St. Paul Pioneer Press-Dispatch

GENE BASSET
Courtesy Atlanta Journal

" I'M BACK IN THE SADDLE AGAIN. "

138

WOULD YOU LIKE:
SMOKING OR NON-SMOKING,
AISLE OR WINDOW,
HARDTOP OR CONVERTIBLE SECTIONS?

139

CLAY BENNETT
Courtesy St. Petersburg Times

WAYNE STAYSKAL
Courtesy Tampa Tribune

"WE HAVE COFFEE, COKE, SPRITE, PEANUTS AND SUPER GLUE!"

140

RE-DISCOVERY

KIRK
©1988 THE BLADE
TOLEDO, OH

KIRK WALTERS
Courtesy Toledo Blade

KEVIN SIERS
Courtesy Charlotte Observer

141

JON KENNEDY
Courtesy Arkansas Democrat

Best supporting actor...

FROM THE VICTIM'S DESCRIPTION WE PRODUCED A COMPOSITE... BUT I DON'T THINK YOU'LL LIKE IT, CHIEF...

STEVE KELLEY
Courtesy San Diego Union

142

The Meese Affair

Special prosecutor Lawrence Walsh launched an investigation in 1986 into Attorney General Edwin Meese's role in the inquiry into the Iran/Contra affair. A year later, Meese's ties to the Wedtech Corporation, a military contractor linked to payoffs of public officials, were the subject of scrutiny by another special prosecutor, James McKay.

After these investigations, however, a grand jury decided there was not enough evidence to indict Meese. The grand jury did add, however, that the evidence raised serious doubts about Meese's judgment. Early in 1988 several high-level officials in the Justice Department resigned, some of them indicating dissatisfaction with Meese's leadership. Democrats began to talk about "the sleaze factor" in the Reagan Administration, and many Republicans admitted it would be best for the party and all concerned if Meese resigned.

Meese announced that since the grand jury report found nothing against him except poor judgment, he therefore had been vindicated. But he resigned from office just before the Republican National Convention.

BOB TAYLOR
Courtesy Dallas Times-Herald

143

ED STEIN
Courtesy Rocky Mountain News

NOW, MR. MEESE, WHEN DID YOU FIRST DISCOVER THAT YOU COULDN'T TELL RIGHT FROM WRONG?

KEN ALEXANDER
Courtesy Copley News

144

ETTA HULME
Courtesy Ft. Worth Star-Telegram

ED GAMBLE
Courtesy Florida Times-Union

"OH, YEAH...WELL I'M NOT GIVING UP WITHOUT A FIGHT! GET ON THE PHONE AND HIRE ME A PR FIRM!"

GIVE ME YOUR ADDICTS... YOUR ILLITERATES... YOUR ANABOLIC STEROID USERS...

JEFF KOTERBA
Courtesy Kansas City Star

I'D LIKE TO GO SOMEWHERE WHERE NOBODY KNOWS ME

BLAINE
Courtesy The Spectator (Ont.)

146

Sports

The 1988 Summer Olympics in Seoul, South Korea, will be remembered not for outstanding athletic performances but for the tragedy of one participant. Ben Johnson, a world-class sprinter, was stripped of his gold medal in the 100-meter dash when tests showed he had used a banned drug. In all, eleven athletes in the Games tested positively for steroids of various kinds.

American diver Greg Louganis hit his head on the springboard during a dive, but came back to win the gold medal in the same event the next day.

Mike Tyson, the world heavyweight boxing champion, continued to demolish all challengers—and to increase his bank account at a record pace. In June, he earned a reported $21.5 million in knocking out Michael Spinks in the first round. Earlier in the year he had kayoed Larry Holmes and Tony Tubbs, earning $12 million for his efforts.

In the America's Cup challenge, Dennis Connor's 60-foot twin-hulled catamaran easily defeated New Zealand's 133-foot single-hulled yacht. The New Zealanders filed suit, contending that it was unfair for a catamaran, which can sail much faster, to compete against a single-hull boat. The New York State Supreme Court was still considering the matter at year's end.

DICK WALLMEYER
Courtesy Long Beach Press-Telegram

147

PAUL FELL
Courtesy Lincoln Journal

A FOOL AND HIS GOLD ARE SOON PARTED....

JERRY BYRD
Courtesy Beaumont Enterprise

$1 MILLION...
$2 MILLION...
$3 MILLION...
$4 MILLION...
$5 MILLION...
$6 MILLION...

JEFF STAHLER
Courtesy Cincinnati Post

MIKE LANE
Courtesy Baltimore Evening Sun

ETTA HULME
Courtesy Ft. Worth Star-Telegram

DREW LITTON
Courtesy Rocky Mountain News

149

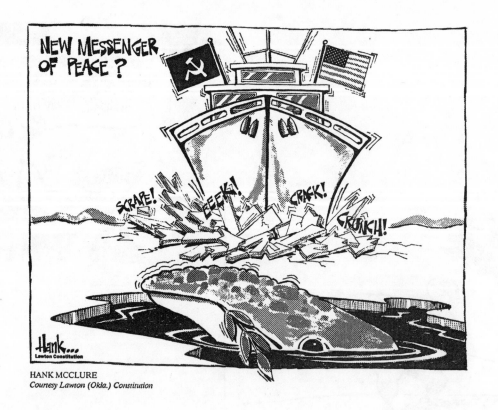

NEW MESSENGER OF PEACE?

SCRAPE! EEEK! CRACK! CRUNCH!

HANK MCCLURE
Courtesy Lawton (Okla.) Constitution

CHARLES ADDAMS Cartoonist 1912-1988

WASSERMAN © '88 BOSTON GLOBE
DIST. BY L.A. TIMES SYND.

DAN WASSERMAN
Courtesy Boston Globe

... and Other Issues

Three gray whales, trapped in the ice off Alaska, captured the attention of the world in late 1988, and a multinational effort costing millions of dollars freed at least two of the beasts and enabled them to escape to the open sea.

A controversial bill in Congress which would have provided federal aid for children's day care failed to make it to the House floor, apparently because of its high cost—some $2.5 billion.

Many famous figures passed from the scene during the year. Among them were: Charles Addams, Henry Armstrong, James Baldwin, Gregory ("Pappy") Boyington, Milton Caniff, Billy Carter, Glenn Cunningham, Price Daniel, Dennis Day, Jascha Heifetz, John Houseman, Trevor Howard, Louis L'Amour, Pete Maravich, John Mitchell, and Franklin D. Roosevelt, Jr.

BEN SARGENT
Courtesy Austin American-Statesman

151

A DAY IN THE LIFE OF RINGO T. CAMSHAFT, THE GUY WHO DESIGNED THE NEW TAX FORMS.

SOUTH AFRICA — WE WANT TO REGISTER OUR DEMANDS FOR A VOICE!

POLAND — WE WANT TO REGISTER OUR DEMANDS FOR A CHOICE!

U.S. — REGISTER TO VOTE?... NO THANKS, I THOUGHT YOU WERE SELLING LOTTERY TICKETS!

LOCK HIM UP! HE WAS HELPING RUNAWAY SLAVES!

LOCK HIM UP! HE WAS HIDING JEWS IN HIS HOUSE!

LOCK HIM UP! HE WAS BLOCKING ENTRY TO AN ABORTION CLINIC!

1858   1938   1988

Welcome to
SOMEWHERE ELSE

Suggested site for
Aids clinics, jails,
Subsidized housing,
& Homes for the retarded

HITCH
WORCESTER TELEGRAM

DAVID HITCH
Courtesy Worcester Telegram-Gazette

DREW LITTON
Courtesy Rocky Mountain News

drew litton...
ROCKY MTN NEWS

"PISTOL" PETE MARAVICH
1947-1988

MIKE LANE
Courtesy Baltimore Evening Sun

GEE, THANKS, SPORT!

#1 DEBTOR

UN

S. C. RAWLS
Courtesy NEA

ADIOS, LOUIS...

STEVE KELLEY
Courtesy San Diego Union

WHEN POLLED ABOUT THE QUESTION OF ADVERTISING CONDOMS ON TELEVISION...

66% OF RESPONDENTS FAVORED THE IDEA...

26% OPPOSED IT...

AND 8% SAID THAT REGARDLESS OF ADS, REAGAN SHOULD CONTINUE TO FUND THE CONDOMS IN NICARAGUA.

154

Then

Now

"HIS MASTER'S VOICE"

SEVERAL BIG CITY NEWSPAPERS HAVE HAD TO SHUT DOWN BECAUSE OF COMPETITION FROM T.V.!

MAYBE VIDEO LEARNS YA STUFF MORE BETTER!

WHAT WOULD YOU DO IF YOU WON A **MILLION DOLLARS?!!?**

RETIRE AND DRIVE ACROSS EUROPE...

PUTT PUTT

..FLY AROUND THE WORLD...

TWA

...BUY NEW CARS...

...OR PERHAPS YOU'D PAY PART OF YOUR KID'S COLLEGE TUITION!!

BILL

COSTELLO ©1988 ASSOCIATED FEATURES THE DIAMONDBACK

I TELL YOU IT WAS TERRIBLE!! MY WORST NIGHTMARE!... I DREAMT JANE FONDA APOLOGIZED FOR GOING TO HANOI AND THAT CARL ROWAN SHOT SOME KID!...

LIBERALS

HANOI JANE: "I'M SORRY"

COLUMNIST SHOOTS INTRUDER

CLYDE WELLS
Courtesy Augusta Chronicle

SCOTT WILLIS
Courtesy San Jose Mercury-News

WORKING MOM SEEKS CHILD CARE

JANE FONDA HAS APOLOGIZED TO VIETNAM VETERANS.

REMIND ME TO WRITE AND THANK HER—15 YEARS FROM NOW...

JACK MCLEOD
Courtesy Army Times

156

Past Award Winners

NATIONAL SOCIETY OF PROFESSIONAL JOURNALISTS AWARD
(Formerly Sigma Delta Chi Award)

1942—Jacob Burck, Chicago Times
1943—Charles Werner, Chicago Sun
1944—Henry Barrow, Associated Press
1945—Reuben L. Goldberg, New York Sun
1946—Dorman H. Smith, NEA
1947—Bruce Russell, Los Angeles Times
1948—Herbert Block, Washington Post
1949—Herbert Block, Washington Post
1950—Bruce Russell, Los Angeles Times
1951—Herbert Block, Washington Post, and
    Bruce Russell, Los Angeles Times
1952—Cecil Jensen, Chicago Daily News
1953—John Fischetti, NEA
1954—Calvin Alley, Memphis Commercial Appeal
1955—John Fischetti, NEA
1956—Herbert Block, Washington Post
1957—Scott Long, Minneapolis Tribune
1958—Clifford H. Baldowski, Atlanta Constitution
1959—Charles G. Brooks, Birmingham News
1960—Dan Dowling, New York Herald-Tribune
1961—Frank Interlandi, Des Moines Register
1962—Paul Conrad, Denver Post
1963—William Mauldin, Chicago Sun-Times
1964—Charles Bissell, Nashville Tennessean
1965—Roy Justus, Minneapolis Star
1966—Patrick Oliphant, Denver Post
1967—Eugene Payne, Charlotte Observer
1968—Paul Conrad, Los Angeles Times
1969—William Mauldin, Chicago Sun-Times
1970—Paul Conrad, Los Angeles Times
1971—Hugh Haynie, Louisville Courier-Journal
1972—William Mauldin, Chicago Sun-Times
1973—Paul Szep, Boston Globe
1974—Mike Peters, Dayton Daily News
1975—Tony Auth, Philadelphia Enquirer
1976—Paul Szep, Boston Globe
1977—Don Wright, Miami News
1978—Jim Borgman, Cincinnati Enquirer
1979—John P. Trever, Albuquerque Journal
1980—Paul Conrad, Los Angeles Times
1981—Paul Conrad, Los Angeles Times
1982—Dick Locher, Chicago Tribune
1983—Rob Lawlor, Philadelphia Daily News
1984—Mike Lane, Baltimore Evening Sun
1985—Doug Marlette, Charlotte Observer
1986—Mike Keefe, Denver Post
1987—Paul Conrad, Los Angeles Times

NATIONAL HEADLINERS CLUB AWARD

1938—C. D. Batchelor, New York Daily News
1939—John Knott, Dallas News
1940—Herbert Block, NEA
1941—Charles H. Sykes, Philadelphia Evening Ledger
1942—Jerry Doyle, Philadelphia Record
1943—Vaughn Shoemaker, Chicago Daily News
1944—Roy Justus, Sioux City Journal
1945—F. O. Alexander, Philadelphia Bulletin
1946—Hank Barrow, Associated Press
1947—Cy Hungerford, Pittsburgh Post-Gazette
1948—Tom Little, Nashville Tennessean
1949—Bruce Russell, Los Angeles Times
1950—Dorman Smith, NEA
1951—C. G. Werner, Indianapolis Star
1952—John Fischetti, NEA
1953—James T. Berryman and
    Gib Crocket, Washington Star
1954—Scott Long, Minneapolis Tribune
1955—Leo Thiele, Los Angeles Mirror-News
1956—John Milt Morris, Associated Press
1957—Frank Miller, Des Moines Register
1958—Burris Jenkins, Jr., New York Journal-American
1959—Karl Hubenthal, Los Angeles Examiner
1960—Don Hesse, St. Louis Globe-Democrat
1961—L. D. Warren, Cincinnati Enquirer
1962—Franklin Morse, Los Angeles Mirror
1963—Charles Bissell, Nashville Tennessean
1964—Lou Grant, Oakland Tribune
1965—Merle R. Tingley, London (Ont.) Free Press
1966—Hugh Haynie, Louisville Courier-Journal
1967—Jim Berry, NEA
1968—Warren King, New York News
1969—Larry Barton, Toledo Blade
1970—Bill Crawford, NEA
1971—Ray Osrin, Cleveland Plain Dealer
1972—Jacob Burck, Chicago Sun-Times
1973—Ranan Lurie, New York Times
1974—Tom Darcy, Newsday
1975—Bill Sanders, Milwaukee Journal
1976—No award given
1977—Paul Szep, Boston Globe
1978—Dwane Powell, Raleigh News and Observer
1979—Pat Oliphant, Washington Star
1980—Don Wright, Miami News
1981—Bill Garner, Memphis Commercial Appeal
1982—Mike Peters, Dayton Daily News
1983—Doug Marlette, Charlotte Observer
1984—Steve Benson, Arizona Republic
1985—Bill Day, Detroit Free Press
1986—Mike Keefe, Denver Post
1987—Mike Peters, Dayton Daily News
1988—Doug Marlette, Charlotte Observer

PAST AWARD WINNERS

PULITZER PRIZE

1922—Rollin Kirby, New York World
1923—No award given
1924—J. N. Darling, New York Herald Tribune
1925—Rollin Kirby, New York World
1926—D. R. Fitzpatrick, St. Louis Post-Dispatch
1927—Nelson Harding, Brooklyn Eagle
1928—Nelson Harding, Brooklyn Eagle
1929—Rollin Kirby, New York World
1930—Charles Macauley, Brooklyn Eagle
1931—Edmund Duffy, Baltimore Sun
1932—John T. McCutcheon, Chicago Tribune
1933—H. M. Talburt, Washington Daily News
1934—Edmund Duffy, Baltimore Sun
1935—Ross A. Lewis, Milwaukee Journal
1936—No award given
1937—C. D. Batchelor, New York Daily News
1938—Vaughn Shoemaker, Chicago Daily News
1939—Charles G. Werner, Daily Oklahoman
1940—Edmund Duffy, Baltimore Sun
1941—Jacob Burck, Chicago Times
1942—Herbert L. Block, NEA
1943—Jay N. Darling, New York Herald Tribune
1944—Clifford K. Berryman, Washington Star
1945—Bill Mauldin, United Feature Syndicate
1946—Bruce Russell, Los Angeles Times
1947—Vaughn Shoemaker, Chicago Daily News
1948—Reuben L. ("Rube") Goldberg, New York Sun
1949—Lute Pease, Newark Evening News
1950—James T. Berryman, Washington Star
1951—Reginald W. Manning, Arizona Republic
1952—Fred L. Packer, New York Mirror
1953—Edward D. Kuekes, Cleveland Plain Dealer
1954—Herbert L. Block, Washington Post
1955—Daniel R. Fitzpatrick, St. Louis Post-Dispatch
1956—Robert York, Louisville Times
1957—Tom Little, Nashville Tennessean
1958—Bruce M. Shanks, Buffalo Evening News
1959—Bill Mauldin, St. Louis Post-Dispatch
1960—No award given
1961—Carey Orr, Chicago Tribune
1962—Edmund S. Valtman, Hartford Times
1963—Frank Miller, Des Moines Register
1964—Paul Conrad, Denver Post
1965—No award given
1966—Don Wright, Miami News
1967—Patrick B. Oliphant, Denver Post
1968—Eugene Gray Payne, Charlotte Observer
1969—John Fischetti, Chicago Daily News
1970—Thomas F. Darcy, Newsday
1971—Paul Conrad, Los Angeles Times
1972—Jeffrey K. MacNelly, Richmond News Leader
1973—No award given
1974—Paul Szep, Boston Globe
1975—Garry Trudeau, Universal Press Syndicate
1976—Tony Auth, Philadelphia Enquirer
1977—Paul Szep, Boston Globe

1978—Jeff MacNelly, Richmond News Leader
1979—Herbert Block, Washington Post
1980—Don Wright, Miami News
1981—Mike Peters, Dayton Daily News
1982—Ben Sargent, Austin American-Statesman
1983—Dick Locher, Chicago Tribune
1984—Paul Conrad, Los Angeles Times
1985—Jeff MacNelly, Chicago Tribune
1986—Jules Feiffer, Universal Press Syndicate
1987—Berke Breathed, Washington Post Writers Group
1988—Doug Marlette, Atlanta Constitution

NATIONAL NEWSPAPER AWARD / CANADA

1949—Jack Boothe, Toronto Globe and Mail
1950—James G. Reidford, Montreal Star
1951—Len Norris, Vancouver Sun
1952—Robert La Palme, Le Devoir, Montreal
1953—Robert W. Chambers, Halifax Chronicle-Herald
1954—John Collins, Montreal Gazette
1955—Merle R. Tingley, London Free Press
1956—James G. Reidford, Toronto Globe and Mail
1957—James G. Reidford, Toronto Globe and Mail
1958—Raoul Hunter, Le Soleil, Quebec
1959—Duncan Macpherson, Toronto Star
1960—Duncan Macpherson, Toronto Star
1961—Ed McNally, Montreal Star
1962—Duncan Macpherson, Toronto Star
1963—Jan Kamienski, Winnipeg Tribune
1964—Ed McNally, Montreal Star
1965—Duncan Macpherson, Toronto Star
1966—Robert W. Chambers, Halifax Chronicle-Herald
1967—Raoul Hunter, Le Soleil, Quebec
1968—Roy Peterson, Vancouver Sun
1969—Edward Uluschak, Edmonton Journal
1970—Duncan Macpherson, Toronto Daily Star
1971—Yardley Jones, Toronto Star
1972—Duncan Macpherson, Toronto Star
1973—John Collins, Montreal Gazette
1974—Blaine, Hamilton Spectator
1975—Roy Peterson, Vancouver Sun
1976—Andy Donato, Toronto Sun
1977—Terry Mosher, Montreal Gazette
1978—Terry Mosher, Montreal Gazette
1979—Edd Uluschak, Edmonton Journal
1980—Vic Roschkov, Toronto Star
1981—Tom Innes, Calgary Herald
1982—Blaine, Hamilton Spectator
1983—Dale Cummings, Winnipeg Free Press
1984—Roy Peterson, Vancouver Sun
1985—Ed Franklin, Toronto Globe and Mail
1986—Brian Gable, Regina Leader Post
1987—Raffi Anderian, Ottawa Citizen

Index

INDEX